ABA
GUIDE TO
ASSISTED REPRODUCTION
TECHNIQUES, LEGAL ISSUES, AND PATHWAYS TO
SUCCESS

JEFFREY A. KASKY & MARLA B. NEUFELD

20 19 18 17 16   5 4 3 2 1

ISBN: 978-1-63425-017-7
e-ISBN: 978-1-63425-018-4

Discounts are available for books ordered in bulk. Special consideration is given to state bars, CLE programs, and other bar-related organizations. Inquire at Book Publishing, ABA Publishing, American Bar Association, 321 N. Clark Street, Chicago, Illinois 60654-7598.

www.shopABA.org

Contents

Introduction

So you want to build a family? Maybe you are a hopeful grandparent or friend holding the hand of a loved one going through a fertility journey. Based on the fact that you are reading this text, we feel safe in guessing that things haven't been going as planned insofar as having a baby the "old-fashioned" way. Or, perhaps you're single or in a same-sex relationship and need medical assistance to start your family.

Well, you came to the right place. Fortunately, with medical advancements, assisted reproductive technology (ART) provides a "new-fashioned way" of building a family. It is now possible to achieve a biological connection to a child for those suffering from the disease of infertility, having medical conditions and/or a risk for passing on inheritable diseases or genetic abnormalities, or for same-sex couples who physically cannot get pregnant without medical intervention. For these parents, ART provides hope, along with the means to have a child through numerous methods, which include insemination, in vitro fertilization, or use of a gestational carrier, just to name a few. These advances in ART technology allow parents to build an immediate family; additionally, ART technology can address an array of medical circumstances. It can be utilized to test the quality of an embryo prior to transfer into the uterus to avoid passing on certain genetic diseases, preserve a person's fertility by freezing eggs, sperm, or embryos for an indefinite amount of time, and allow for conception of a genetic child after the source of the genetic material is deceased or incapacitated.

Medical advancements do not occur in a vacuum; great strides in ART technology come with equally rapid changes in the legal arena at both state and constitutional levels. Complex and novel issues are constantly evolving with ART legal implications, such as how parental rights are determined with newly formed nontraditional families, how to balance the rights of the parties involved in ART, as well as how to define issues surrounding the legal definitions of parenthood. The legal reaction to ART around the world is vast and varied, and is shaped by societal values coupled with different interpretations of laws and regulations.

The *ABA Guide to Assisted Reproduction* is the A to Z of ART. It is an insider's guide to available ART options. This guide is designed to educate anyone considering an ART procedure (that's you) in the processes involved in choosing medical providers, legal representatives, and other key players throughout the ART journey, as well as understanding the protocol to enter into appropriate legal contracts while addressing the unique issues that may arise pre- and postbirth. It also provides insider tips and tricks from professionals well versed in the ART industry, such as renowned fertility physicians, embryologists, attorneys, mental health professionals, and those who have personally been through their own ART experiences, just to name a few, to help traverse what can be a mine field of issues.

The authors of this book are attorneys Jeffrey A. Kasky and Marla B. Neufeld. Jeffrey has operated a successful surrogacy and adoption service for several years, and Marla practices ART law based on her legal expertise coupled with her personal experience of using a surrogate to build her own family.

The sheer amount of data, opinions, theories, advice, medical literature, and legal guidance available can be overwhelming and, at times, even inaccurate. The coauthors have combined their professional and personal experiences to separate the wheat from the chaff in order to provide an easily digestible guide for the fertility layman.

There is no law, nor is there anything in the US Constitution, that guarantees that you'll be able to be a parent to children. That being said, as profoundly stated by John F. Kennedy, "Things do not happen. Things are made to happen." This saying could not be more true that building a family through means of ART. While the path to parenthood through ART may not be straightforward and requires expending time, money, energy, and mental resources, this book will help simply guide you through the impressive array of options that are all designed to help you start your family to "make things happen," as Kennedy encourages.

The Authors and Their Experience with ART

Marla B. Neufeld

I was under the impression that once you decide to start a family, you toss the birth control and give it the "old college try." Poof! There you are booking your family cruise. I was surely mistaken. The reality: my husband and I suffered through years of failed fertility treatments, disappointment, and expense. We attempted intrauterine insemination (IUI) and in vitro fertilization (IVF); I injected boxes of hormones, took steroids, blood thinners, and endured multiple miscarriages. Ultimately we had success with the use of a gestational surrogate who carried and gave birth to our beautiful twin boys. While the journey was challenging, both emotionally and financially, looking back I certainly have had a few laughs along the way at the extremes we endured to build our family.

In addition to the medical ART efforts, we tried everything under the sun that people told us worked to try and get pregnant. I ventured boosting my fertility by motley methods. I diagnosed myself with celiac disease and avoided all gluten solely based on a friend that had fertility success by eliminating gluten. Fast forward six months and by then gluten free was "so two IVF cycles ago!" I saw an acupuncturist and digested pungent Chinese herbs; at his suggestion I avoided all cold food and beverages, as Eastern cultures believe that cold foods make an unpleasant environment for implantation of an embryo.

I carried with me fertility good luck charms spanning the globe from Africa, Japan, and China. I had a sage expert come to my house and smoke out our entire home with sage in an attempt to rid it of evil spirits. I participated in multiple *mikvah* baths, which in Judaism are a religious cleansing bath thought to increase fertility. I even experimented with the supernatural by going to a psychic and tarot card reader to see if there were children in our future.

As a creative effort, and after my fertility doctor told me that certain creams/shampoos can negatively impact my hormones, instead of brown bagging all my beauty products to my next appointment, I made him a creative collage of the products by artistically placing the labels on a board so he could review the ingredients. I now have multiple mystery bottles of label-less creams and soaps from this investigation. Needless to say, one of these good luck charms eventually worked; maybe it was good that I tried all of them.

Backing up a bit as to how we arrived at our plan of action: After numerous fertility treatments and multiple miscarriages, we reached a baby-making crossroad and had to reassess our game plan. We had several frozen embryos remaining from a prior cycle. I could try IVF again by means of a frozen embryo transfer (FET), but as much as I wanted to be pregnant and carry our baby to term, my chances of success were very slim. Ultimately our fertility doctor approved us for surrogacy.

Although my husband was thrilled to see me stop taking fertility medications, I was initially unsettled with the decision. My pregnant friends made comments like, "At least you won't get fat or have morning sickness." Those who have never experienced IVF have no idea how frustrating this is to hear. Although this was initially upsetting, I knew their hearts were in the right place and eventually learned how to take their comments in stride.

The surrogacy journey moved forward. It took six months to find a surrogacy agency, surrogate, attorney, finalize medical and psychological testing, and finish the surrogacy contract. During that time, I was able to process everything and was excited about the opportunity. Financial concerns are of paramount importance as surrogacy can range from $60,000 to $150,000 plus. Some expenses include medical costs for IVF; medications; two attorneys: one to write the contract and one to review for the surrogate; surrogate agency fee; medical insurance for the surrogate; and reasonable living expenses of the surrogate. These factors will be addressed in great detail in the pages that follow.

Prior to my infertility experience, I practiced only transactional law. My infertility/surrogacy journey inspired me to branch out my practice to include surrogacy and reproductive technology law, awarding me the pleasure of helping others. I know firsthand that surrogacy is daunting and I can now help others navigate through the system to understand the process and the legal implications. As a fun side note, we are among celebrities that have ventured down the surrogacy road such as Jimmy Fallon, Sarah Jessica Parker, Ellen Pompeo, and Elton John to name a few. We received unbelievable support from our family, friends, community and new surrogacy family to help make what seemed impossible become a reality. As my surrogate always said, "It takes teamwork to make the dream work."

Throughout this journey, my husband and I and our supportive family and friends have grown closer; you truly learn the quality of a relationship when tested with a challenge. This experience shaped my career in inspiring me to practice reproductive technology law, which will ultimately help others through infertility. I never would have imagined this scenario but intend to turn it into a positive, constructive path. I look forward to sharing my knowledge and helping others fulfill their dreams. As it relates to my ART journey both personally and professionally, special thank you to my supportive husband for being strong for me through the difficulties we faced, my loving and adorable sister, my amazingly wonderful parents—without them, none of this would have ever been possible, my co-author Jeff (and the incredible Jeannette), who shared this writing opportunity with me and made the challenge of writing a book fun, and my boys who make me laugh and smile every single day and inspire me to continue to help other people build a family through ART. Lastly, to my surrogate whose positive outlook on life carried me through my ART journey.

Jeffrey A. Kasky

When I was a kid, growing up with my sister (who still insists she's an only child) and my parents, who were only twenty-one years older than I, my plan was forged early: two kids, close in age to each other, and DONE. How adorable of me to think I had any say in the matter!

Through twists and turns, ups and downs, I am now the proud father of four, consisting of three boys and one girl. Suffice it to say I never had to personally deal with the let-downs and struggles that so many of my readers and clients have had to live through. On the contrary, until I met up with Dr. David Weinstein and his scalpel for my two vasectomies (yeah, it took two), I was a little *over*-blessed with fertility.

My first surrogacy case came to me by accident. A colleague who knew I did adoptions assumed I knew anything about how to handle a surrogacy. Never the one to turn down the opportunity to help, I took the case, learned all I could as quickly as possible, and helped a nice couple become parents of triplets. Now, having lost count of how many cases I've worked on and babies born to my clients, I can honestly say that it's my favorite area of law.

It is my sincere hope that whatever your reason for reading this book, your expectations—if not your hopes and dreams—are thoroughly fulfilled. Just keep in mind that there is no law that says that everyone who wants to be a parent automatically gets to be a parent. As you have likely already seen, it takes a strong will and perseverance, not to mention a big fat bank account, to succeed in this arena. Nor is it required by law that just because you become an adult and perhaps marry, you are required to procreate or otherwise raise children. I can't tell you how many people I've met over the years who were seeking to start a family based on pressure from family and friends. I'd be lying if I said that I don't sometimes admire my friends who've chosen to earn a living and enjoy it for themselves.

All right, with all of that said, let me add the following important fact, and then I'll let you get to the good stuff. This book was primarily written by my coauthor, the brilliant and lovely Marla B. Neufeld, Esq. I contributed some materials and some editorial effort, but I'd be more like an executive producer or director, as opposed to the writer, if this were a film. That said, nothing happens without teamwork, and I appreciate the contributions that were made by everyone involved.

Disclaimer

This book was written and is being presented by lawyers. As such, you would likely have been shocked had there not been a thorough disclaimer right here in the beginning. With that said:

We, the authors, are lawyers, but we are not your lawyers. The text herein is not intended to be legal advice from a lawyer to a client. The only type of "advice" offered herein is based on the authors' personal and professional experience, and is to be considered anecdotally. Under no circumstances should these contents be considered to be or used as a substitute for hiring competent and experienced professionals to represent you and advocate for you.

This book is aptly referred to as a "guide" to ART. While many reputable professionals have contributed to this book and provided invaluable insight, it is not to be viewed as definitive legal, medical, or psychological advice for the readers. Please consider this book as an empowering tool to help guide you through the maze of the ART world. The best specific advice (nonlegal) we can give you is that as you embark upon your family-building journey, engage the appropriate professionals along the way to provide the customized guidance you need.

It is important to remember that when dealing with ART, each state and country (for international clients) has its own specific laws (or lack thereof) relating to issues such as egg, sperm, and embryo donation and surrogacy. In some states it is a crime to compensate a surrogate for carrying a child, while in others there is a structured statutory framework in place governing the ART processes. Therefore, it is imperative that when you engage in a form of ART, you consult with an attorney licensed in your state to determine the applicable regulations, if any, and avoid the myriad disastrous legal pitfalls that can occur.

Since we can't create a time machine to see what the future holds relating to ART laws, by the time this book is published, the information and laws may have changed, thereby reinforcing reason to consult with a legal professional when embarking upon your ART journey.

Medical Implications

Overview of ART Medical Procedures

Considered one of the top major medical advances in the past sixty-five years, on par with the creation of antibiotics, the advent of assisted reproductive technology (ART), including in vitro fertilization (IVF), has changed the way people create families. Noncoital? No problem. With the advent of ART, it is amazing how many numerous options there are whereby people can create a family without ever having intercourse. It is now possible that a mother can carry and give birth to her child without having provided the genetics (egg donation); a couple can have a child who is carried by the mother but is genetically related to neither parent (embryo donation); an individual or couple can have a child to whom they are both genetically related yet a third party gives birth to the child (gestational surrogacy), just to name a few of these possibilities. While attempts at IVF date back to the 1890s with the first reported case of an embryo transfer in rabbits, the birth (pun intended) of IVF occurred in 1978 in the United Kingdom, where Lesley Brown and her husband, John, had failed to conceive after attempting pregnancy for nine years. Without conducting any type of egg stimulation, Lesley underwent laparoscopic egg retrieval. British physiologist Robert Geoffrey Edwards took Lesley's husband's sperm and fertilized the retrieved egg in the lab. A few days later, an eight-cell stage embryo was transferred inside Lesley's uterine cavity. At 11:47 p.m. on July 25, 1978, 5 lb. 12 oz. Louise Brown, who was then called a "test tube baby," was safely delivered by cesarean section. (Fun fact: Louise eventually went on to have her own child conceived naturally.) By the birth of Louise Brown, the world celebrated what was once an in-"conceivable" feat. A new era of assisted human reproductive technology has now contributed to more than 5 million babies conceived through IVF around the world.

Medical Procedures for Intended Parents

Preconception Health: Get Healthy Before Getting a Belly

Before trying to get pregnant with ART, many clinics evaluate both men and women to help maximize chances for fertility success and a healthy pregnancy. Good preconception health is essential to achieving pregnancy with ART. Chronic medical conditions such as diabetes, hypertension, and asthma should be addressed before attempting to conceive.

Like finding the perfect temperature for the bears' porridge in *Goldilocks and the Three Bears*, you can't be too skinny or too fat for an ideal pregnancy outcome . . . you have to be *just* right!

A healthy weight, with a normal body mass index (BMI) between 20 and 24 is critical for a higher success of conception and is key to maintaining a healthy pregnancy. According to reproductive endocrinologist Dr. Kenneth M. Gelman, affiliated with the South Florida Institute for Reproductive Medicine (SFIRM) (http://www.ivfmd.com), a patient is considered "obese" with a BMI over 30, and at SFIRM no patient can conduct IVF if the BMI is over 40 as the risks to the patient can include higher chances of miscarriage and complications during pregnancy. It is important to remember that a BMI can also be too low, and Dr. Gelman recommends keeping a BMI above 20 for ideal pregnancy success.

In addition to a healthy weight, Dr. Gelman counsels his patients who are considering pregnancy to refrain from smoking or drinking alcohol in excess and to cut down on caffeine. Eating a healthy diet—such as the Mediterranean-type diet that is rich in foods like fruits, vegetables, beans, fish, and olive oil—is as important as pursuing healthy activities such as yoga or acupuncture. It is also essential to take the recommended doses of prenatal vitamins, which include folic acid and docosahexaenoic acid (DHA), to prevent birth defects and support brain development.

Getting ready for pregnancy? Follow this guide to preconception health according to the March of Dimes, an organization helping moms have full-term pregnancies and healthy babies:

Take folic acid. Take a multivitamin with 400 micrograms of folic acid in it each day as part of healthy eating. Folic acid is a B vitamin that every cell in your body needs for healthy growth and development. If you take it before and during early pregnancy, it may help protect your baby from birth defects of the brain and spine.

Get a preconception checkup. This is a medical checkup to help make sure you're as healthy as you can be before you get pregnant. It's one of the best things you can do for you and your baby. This checkup helps your healthcare provider make sure that your body is ready for pregnancy. Your provider can spot and assist you managing and sometimes preventing certain health conditions, like obesity and certain infections that may affect your chances of getting pregnant as well as the health of your baby during pregnancy.

Make healthy choices. It may take some work for you and your partner to change habits or your lifestyle to improve your chances of getting pregnant and having a healthy baby. Here's what you can do:

- Don't smoke, drink alcohol, or take street drugs. All of these can affect your fertility and your baby once you get pregnant. Tell your provider if you need help to quit.
- Take prescription drugs exactly as your provider says to. Make sure any provider who prescribes you medicine knows that you're trying to get pregnant. When you take any medicine, don't take more than your provider says you can take, don't take it with alcohol or other drugs, and don't take anyone else's prescription medicine.
- Get to a healthy weight. Eat healthy foods and do something active every day. An unhealthy weight can affect your fertility. When you do get pregnant, being under- or overweight can cause problems for your baby, like being born too early or too small. Talk to your provider about your BMI. Eat healthy foods and be active. Do things that you and your partner can do together, like going for walks. You don't have to join a gym to be healthy.
- Find out about harmful chemicals you use at home or work. Ask your provider if they can affect your chances of getting pregnant or your baby when you do get pregnant.
- Lower your stress. Thinking about fertility treatment may make you feel nervous or scared. This can be a lot of stress to add to your life. High levels of stress can cause problems during pregnancy, so it's a good idea to find ways to manage stress before you get pregnant. Being active, eating healthily, and getting plenty of sleep can alleviate stress. If you're really stressed out, tell your provider who can refer you to a counselor to help you reduce and handle your stress.

Get into Your Genes: Genetic Testing Considerations Prior to or During Pregnancy

In preparing to have a baby, you may purchase adorable baby jeans. You also may want to consider researching your *genetic genes* prior to pregnancy or during ART procedures.

The Victor Center for the Prevention of Jewish Genetic Diseases provides outreach, education, and affordable genetic counseling and screening for Jewish genetic diseases (JGDs) to young adults considering having children. For more information on preconception screening, you can check out your genes by checking out http://www.victorcenter.org.

According to Deborah Z. Wasserman, MS, of the Nicklaus Children's Hospital's Miami Victor Center and Faye L. Shapiro, MS, LCGC, of the Einstein Medical Center Philadelphia's Victor Center, a genetic counselor is a health care professional who works closely with obstetricians and medical geneticists to provide risk assessment and counseling for couples at risk for having a baby with a birth defect or genetic condition. A genetic counselor will obtain information about your family history, medical history and pregnancy history. The counselor will explain the risks to the pregnancy, if any, based on these histories, as well as any options available for preconception testing and prenatal diagnosis. The risks, benefits, and limitations of prenatal diagnosis are reviewed, such that the couple has all the information they need to make an informed decision regarding testing. Since some scenarios can be more complicated than others, the genetic counselor may be a valuable member of the obstetrics team in helping ensure that all available testing is offered and that all necessary testing gets done.

If you are wondering whether you should consult with a genetic counselor prior to getting pregnant, Wasserman and Shapiro share the following reasons a person may wish to talk to a genetic counselor when considering building a family:

- Family history of a genetic issue
- Past pregnancy history of two or more miscarriages, a stillbirth, or infant death to help determine the cause of the losses and possible recurrence risks
- Advanced maternal age
- Maternal medical conditions such as diabetes or epilepsy
- Medications during pregnancy that can cause serious birth defects
- Ethnic background that poses a higher risk of being a carrier for specific genetic diseases, such as sickle cell disease in African Americans or Tay-Sachs disease and others in Jewish people.

There is also genetic screenings and diagnostic testing that can be performed during pregnancy. According to Wasserman and Shapiro, such screening and diagnostic testing during pregnancy includes:

- Maternal serum screening: First trimester, second trimester, or a combination of the two
- Noninvasive Prenatal Testing (NIPT): This can be done early in a pregnancy (as early as nine weeks)
- Ultrasound: First trimester nuchal measurement and second trimester anatomy scan
- Fetal echocardiogram: A special ultrasound focusing on the baby's heart
- Fetal MRI: May be used to clarify ultrasound findings
- Chorionic villi sampling (CVS): A tiny amount of tissue from the outside of the placenta (which comes from the same fertilized egg as the baby) is obtained for analysis
- Amniocentesis: A small amount of fluid is withdrawn from the sac around the baby, and this fluid contains skin cells that have been shed by the baby. From the cells obtained from both CVS and amniocentesis, chromosomes can be analyzed to rule out conditions like Down syndrome (an extra copy of chromosome #21), and DNA can be isolated for the possible diagnosis of a particular condition known to run in that family
- PUBS (umbilical cord blood sampling)

Getting Organized for ART

It's hard to know where to start when preparing for your first appointment with a reproductive doctor. Dr. Gelman recommends bringing the following information to maximize your visit:

- Obstetrical and gynecological records
- Current Papanicolaou test (Pap smear)
- Mammogram records
- Other applicable records from other providers in the field to see what tests/procedures have been conducted
- Your partner (if applicable)

Before embarking into an ART procedure, Dr. Gelman says that the typical screening process for a new patient considering ART starts with reviewing their medical history. If a couple is considering ART, it is important to conduct a thorough review of the medical history of both parties to determine specific issues and to chart the best course for a couple.

Following a review of the patients' medical history, the physician performs an ultrasound to look at the woman's uterus, ovaries, and anatomy. On the third day of the woman's menstrual cycle, she has blood work done to test her anti-Mullerian hormone (AMH) levels. The AMH levels are thought to reflect the size of a woman's remaining egg supply, which is her ovarian reserve. Additional tests via blood work are conducted to test a woman's thyroid and prolactin levels and to screen for certain genetic conditions such as cystic fibrosis and fragile X syndrome; other genetics tests may be indicated. A standard Food and Drug Administration (FDA) panel of tests are conducted on both members of a couple considering ART to check for diseases such a hepatitis, HIV, and syphilis. A semen analysis is performed on the male partner to check his sperm quantity and quality. Following the initial blood work, the fertility clinic performs anatomic testing such as a hysterosalpingogram (HSG) (a catheter is inserted into the uterus and the fallopian tubes to ensure there are no blockages), an endometrial biopsy, or scraping, to make sure the uterus is healthy, and a saline sonohysterogram (ultrasound to look at the inside of your uterus using a salt (saline) solution for a clearer image) to determine whether there are endometrial polyps or fibroids within the uterus.

Intrauterine Insemination (IUI)

Artificial insemination, dating back to its first usage in 1790, is one of the original old-fashioned ways to conceive (although perhaps not as old as intercourse) and is one of many methods used for treating infertility. Intrauterine insemination (IUI) is a form of artificial insemination that can be done within a clinical setting with the assistance of a physician or can be done at home through a method colloquially referred to as the "turkey baster" method.

When this procedure occurs at a fertility clinic, sperm that have been tested, washed, and concentrated are placed directly in a woman's uterus around the time the woman ovulates, releasing one or more eggs to be fertilized. This procedure is typically reserved for the intended mother and not a surrogate, thus avoiding a genetic connection to the child. The woman is monitored by way of ultrasound and/or blood tests to monitor her cycle of ovulation and to conduct the transfer at the ideal time. The procedure is generally painless and quick. Following the transfer, a doctor may have the woman lie down for a few minutes to let the sperm settle into her body. The ideal outcome of IUI is for sperm to swim into the fallopian tube and hopefully fertilize a waiting egg, thus resulting in conception. Depending on the reasons for infertility, IUI can be coordinated with a "natural" cycle where one egg is released or it can be done in conjunction with fertility medications where multiple eggs are produced and released for hopeful fertilization.

When an IUI is conducted at home, a woman self-inseminates with a man's sperm, using a syringe or other injectable device, and shoots the sperm into her body. At-home insemination can raise medical risks as the source of the sperm, which at times is provided by a friend, may not be stringently tested like it would be in a medical setting. Additionally, while all ART procedures raise novel legal questions, the process of at-home insemination is fraught with legal concerns. For instance, the parties may not realize the importance of having the proper legal documents in place to ensure that the donor relinquishes his rights to the sperm and resulting child. Nothing is worse than a sperm donor thinking he is helping a couple start a family and then getting slapped with a paternity lawsuit years down the road. Or, in the alternative, it can't be pleasant to be led to believe that you'll have a place in the life of a child who was created with your own DNA, only to find that there was never a plan to include you in his future. Notably, the majority of reported legal cases in the United States relate to legal challenges stemming from donated sperm.

For any form of IUI, the source of the sperm can be from the intended father, a donor—either a known or anonymous—donor, or it can be a "blended IUI" where the sperm of the intended father is blended with that of a donor. Blending can help to increase the success rate if the intended father has low sperm count or, as seen with same-sex male couples, to let the strongest swimming sperm decide who will be the genetic parent.

In Vitro Fertilization (IVF)

According to the Society for Assisted Reproductive Technology (SART), approximately 99 percent of ART cycles performed are IVF. SART provides in its *Patient's Guide to Assisted Reproductive Technology* that "for patients under 30, success rates of 30–50% per oocyte retrieval can legitimately be expected; for patients over 40, realistic success rates are only 5% to at most 20%."[1]

When comparing IUI to IVF, Dr. Kenneth Gelman says that "hands down," IVF is more successful than IUI; well over double the success as seen with IUI.

Dr. Gelman agrees that the main factors that assist in a successful IVF cycle are the age of the woman and quality of her egg. If egg quality is poor and the woman is older, the chances of pregnancy success are lower; egg quality begins to decrease at age 35.

---

[1] http://www.sart.org/Patients_Guide.

The process of IVF may seem daunting and overwhelming. However, when you break the process down into steps, it becomes a lot more manageable. Many fertility clinics provide detailed calendars and schedules for the IVF process and include updated reminders as the process progresses. This helps reduce the stress one may feel when inundated with vast amounts of medical information. The basic steps in an IVF treatment cycle are (i) ovarian stimulation, (ii) removing the eggs (egg retrieval), (iii) fertilization of the egg and sperm, (iv) embryo transfer into the uterus, (v) cryopreservation or freezing the embryos, and (vi) pregnancy test.

Ovarian Stimulation (creation of eggs)

What came first, the chicken or the egg? Those in the ART world would certainly say the egg through the process of IVF.

The process of stimulating the ovaries (either of the intended mother or of an egg donor) is called *ovarian stimulation* or *ovulation induction*. Since a woman typically only produces one egg each month, without medical intervention, during this phase the woman is prescribed a cocktail of fertility medications to stimulate her body to produce multiple eggs.

During the ovarian stimulation process, a patient prepares herself for numerous visits to the fertility clinic, as the ovaries are monitored periodically with vaginal ultrasound and hormone levels are monitored by way of blood tests to watch the progression of the creation of the eggs. As the eggs get larger, the patient's appointments with the doctors increase because the timing of the egg retrieval is critical. A typical ovarian stimulation process lasts eight to fourteen days.

Egg Retrieval (removing the eggs)

The egg retrieval process is an involved medical procedure under the guidance of a skilled IVF physician and embryolgist. According to embryologist Dr. Michael B. Matilsky, Ph.D., H.C.L.D., the IVF laboratory director at Boca Fertility (http://www.bocafertility.com):

> Most IVF patients never meet the embryologist, who plays a crucial role in their fertility treatment. However, there is much to learn in the IVF laboratory. After a woman finishes her ovarian hyperstimulation to bring a number of primordial follicles (ovarian cell complexes each of which contain a single egg) to maturation, she is brought to the operating room so that the reproductive endocrinologist can remove the eggs from each individual follicle. This procedure is accomplished under light intravenous (IV) sedation and takes approximately 15–20 minutes. Each large follicle is punctured by an ultrasound-guided needle and the follicular fluid is aspirated into test tubes which are brought to the IVF laboratory. The embryologist then empties each test tube into large petri dishes and searches for the cumulus complex (follicular cells which envelope each egg). The average number of retrieved eggs is usually 10–12, but each woman reacts to the hormonal medications differently and the egg count is dependent on many factors, including age, hormonal status, sensitivity to medication, etc. The range in my IVF lab is from 0 to 55 eggs retrieved.

Fertilization of the Egg and Sperm

How are the egg and sperm fertilized? Imagine the opening scene from the 1989 movie *Look Who's Talking* where John Travolta's sperm, among millions of sperm, raced to fertilize Kirstie Alley's egg to the tune of the Beach Boys' song *I Get Around*. The only similarity IVF has to this iconic scene is that the Beach Boys' song might be playing in the lab, while an embryologist, like Dr. Matilsky, would be doing the fertilization.

Embryo Transfer into a Uterus

The day of the embryo transfer is nerve-racking. This is the day that the embryos you worked so hard on creating are transferred into the uterus of either the intended mother or the surrogate.

The embryo transfer process is relatively simple and painless; some women are prescribed a mild sedative for the procedure, even if just to relax their nerves on this big day. According to embryologist Dr. Michael B. Matilsky's perspective from under the microscope: "The embryo transfer is accomplished using a tiny catheter attached to a tiny syringe. The chosen embryos are aspirated by the embryologist into the catheter in approximately 0.3 of one milliliter. The catheter is then guided through the cervical canal by the doctor using ultrasound to help find the best spot in the uterine cavity to deposit the fluid containing the embryo(s)."

People think of IVF and have images of *Jon and Kate Plus 8,* or, heaven forbid, the dreaded "Octomom," with multiple children being born as a result of fertility treatments. While in the United States there is no objective *legal* restraint on the number of embryos transferred per cycle, the American Society for Reproductive Medicine (ASRM), establishes guidelines (with no force of law) on how many embryos *should* be transferred into a woman based on multiple factors such as age, embryo quality, and other individual patient and embryo characteristics. The guidelines establishing embryo transfer limits have been effective in helping US ART programs maintain their high success rates while significantly decreasing the number of risky multiple pregnancies (triplets and higher). The reproductive endocrinologist or embryologist will discuss this with the patient prior to the transfer.

Dr. Gelman says that typically patients transfer one or two embryos, maximum, with the rare exception for older individuals over 40 and having suffered multiple IVF failures to transfer three embryos. The number of embryos transferred depends on various factors such as the patients' preference on having multiples, whether a patient would consider selective reduction if more than two embryos implant, or coexisting medical conditions such as uterine anomalies, as it may not be advisable for a woman to carry multiples.

Does transferring two embryos double your chances of pregnancy success? Dr. Gelman says no. Transferring two embryos, over one embryo, only increases your chance of pregnancy success by 15–20 percent. According to Dr. Gelman, if you take 100 women in their early 30s and by way of IVF transferred three embryos in each of these women, 50 percent of the women would get pregnant.

Of the 50 percent of pregnant women, about 67 percent of these women would be pregnant with a singleton, 32 percent would be pregnant with twins, and 3 percent would be pregnant with triplets. When considering transferring more than one embryo, you have to consider the risks that Dr. Gelman warns against such as premature birth. Typically twins are one month premature, and triplets are two months premature. Premature birth can cause medical issues for the children such as developmental anomalies, birth defects, cerebral hemorrhages, and poor lung and vision development, just to name a few examples.

Cryopreservation (Freezing the Embryos)

After the embryo transfer, there is the possibility that quality embryos remain that can be cryopreserved (or frozen) for possible use at a later cycle.

As to the potential risks to the child of using frozen embryos, according to the American Society for Reproductive Medicine,[2] "there have been no documented cases of infectious disease transmission, nor do the risks or birth defects, chromosomal anomalies, or pregnancy complications appear to be increased compared

NOTE

Reports have shown that embryos can be frozen for up to twenty years and used successfully, resulting in a live birth.

with using fresh sperm, eggs, or embryos." There are various methods on how embryos are frozen based on the fertility clinic's procedures.

The Pregnancy Test

Now comes the hard part (as if everything else leading up to this point wasn't hard enough!). After the IVF cycle is complete, the intended parents have to endure the two-week wait from the date of the embryo transfer to find out if they are pregnant. Fertility doctors say to stay away from the at-home pregnancy tests as several days are required for the fertilized egg to implant into the uterus and start emitting enough hormones to be detected by the test. There is the chance that the fertility hormones may cause an incorrect outcome, showing either a false positive or negative, yet many women cannot resist taking the at-home tests. The official pregnancy test is performed via a blood test. The blood pregnancy test is frequently called a "beta" as the test measures a beta chain portion of the hCG hormone molecule and is officially named a "beta hCG" test.

If the pregnancy results are negative, it can be a severe blow to the intended parents and everyone else involved. They want to know why it didn't work and many times there are no answers. Following a negative test, the intended parents are instructed to stop the fertility medications and schedule a follow-up appointment with the fertility doctor to map out a new game plan. The wait time before a new cycle can begin is usually about a month or two, depending on various factors.

---

[2] https://www.asrm.org/Assisted_Reproductive_Technologies_booklet/.

Medical Procedures for a Surrogate

Before the intended parents execute a contract with a surrogate, the surrogate is initially medically screened by the reproductive doctor to make sure she is a safe candidate (i.e., free of communicable diseases and otherwise medically fit). The screening will, of course, address and hopefully confirm that the prospective surrogate's reproductive organs are functioning properly. The standard timeframe from the moment a surrogate first visits the fertility clinic for her initial work up until the embryo is transferred is approximately three to four months.

A typical medical work up for a surrogate begins at the start of her menstrual cycle and includes a baseline ultrasound; a hysteroscopy, which looks into her uterine cavity to ensure it looks normal; communicable and preconception blood work for the surrogate and, depending on the fertility clinic, her husband/partner; a urine drug screen; and an annual exam with a Pap smear and herpes culture. Additionally, a consultation with a nurse or doctor is scheduled to discuss the medical processes and medications involved, as well as to answer any questions. It is helpful to obtain the surrogate's prior pregnancy medical records and current Pap smear results for the reproductive physician to analyze during her initial work up. Synched up to the surrogate's period, the fertility clinic may perform a "mock cycle," which is essentially a dry run whereby the physician practices doing the embryo transfer to ensure they know the optimal path to the surrogate's uterus.

During the surrogate's medical review, she needs to read and sign off on any applicable forms at the fertility clinic relating to consent for the medical procedures and risks involved. The FDA has established mandatory regulations for IVF patients that require testing of the parties providing the egg or the sperm (either the intended parents or any sperm or egg donor) and testing of the surrogate and, if applicable, her partner or spouse. The FDA's stringent regulations are to decrease communicable disease exposure to the surrogate and the resulting child. Even before the contract is finalized and signed, some fertility clinics allow the surrogate to start her required birth control pill protocol. Once the surrogacy contract is signed, the surrogate can begin her daily fertility injection medications or other type of medications that prepare her endometrium (uterine lining) to be nice and thick for the transfer of the embryo. The intended parents pay for all of the IVF procedures and medications for the surrogate.

While it may seem counterintuitive to give the surrogate birth control when trying to get her pregnant, a surrogate is placed on birth control initially for a couple of weeks. The first medication the surrogate injects is typically leuprolide acetate (Lupron), which is injected into her abdominal area on a daily basis. This medication suppresses ovulation and ensures the surrogate will not release her own egg. After approximately eight to twelve days of Lupron, along with blood tests to continually check her hormone levels, the surrogate begins taking estrogen, which stimulates the grown of the uterine lining, and she then starts administering progesterone (either a cream or a muscular injection) to prepare the uterine lining for the implantation of the embryos. Other medications may be needed for the surrogate depending on the individual circumstances. While taking these medications, the surrogate is required to perform multiple ultrasounds and blood tests to see how she is responding to the medications and to perfectly time the date for the embryo transfer. In addition to the medical testing, the surrogate is psychologically analyzed as discussed in this book.

Unless the intended parents are using a traditional surrogate with the surrogate's own egg (not recommended!), the intended parents are working on the creation of the embryo simultaneously with the medical processes happening for the surrogate to get her screened and ready for the embryo transfer. The intended parents may have frozen embryos ready and waiting for the transfer, they may be cycling the intended mother to do an egg retrieval to use her egg, or they may engage an egg donor to retrieve her egg and create the embryo to be transferred into the surrogate.

Administering a surrogacy journey is a fertility puzzle being put together by all the parties involved, which culminates at the embryo transfer into the surrogate.

Once the embryos are created and the surrogate's uterus is fluffy like a cloud and ready to be the future home to the embryos, the embryo transfer is performed. What follows is the dreaded two-week wait, at the end of which the parties find out whether or not a pregnancy has been achieved.

Medical Procedures for Egg Donors

Upon becoming a patient at a fertility clinic, an egg donor must sign the required forms consenting to the egg retrieval and acknowledge the medical risks involved. A thorough evaluation or screening of an egg donor is of critical importance for the safety of the donor, intended parents, possible surrogate, and future child, whether the donor is known to the recipient (for example, a family member) or is anonymous.

The FDA strictly regulates the required testing, supported by clinical evidence. Before an egg donor can provide her eggs to an intended parent, she is tested to ensure that she is free of any infections caused by relevant communicable disease agents and communicable diseases. The egg donor is checked for a variety of diseases and conditions such as hepatitis, HIV, syphilis, drug use, chlamydia, etc. Genetic screening both via a detailed family history and specific blood tests, which are determined by her ethnic/racial background, is conducted to determine the presence of issues such as cystic fibrosis, Tay-Sachs disease, sickle cell disease, thalassemia, etc. The egg donor also undergoes a fertility evaluation to verify the capacity of the ovaries to produce eggs, and certain cultures are examined; additionally a physical examination and pelvic ultrasound are performed. In addition to the medical testing, the egg donor is psychologically analyzed as discussed within this book.

Simultaneous with the medical processes happening for the egg donor, which are preparing her to be screened and ready for the egg retrieval, the intended parents may be looking for a sperm donor, and either the intended mother or surrogate are simultaneously preparing their uterus for the embryo transfer. Once the egg donor passes the required screening, the process of retrieving her eggs is the same as the IVF egg retrieval procedures for the intended mother.

IVF Soup, a Mixture of Combinations for Creating Families with IVF

The advent of IVF allows people to build a family with a possible genetic connection who may not otherwise be able to do so, either because of infertility struggles or just anatomical impossibilities as with same-sex couples. It's amazing to consider what seems to be an endless combination of the new dimension of life-giving options with the use of ART, which include:

- Same-sex female partners use IUI or IVF to get pregnant in one of the female partners with the use of a sperm donor (anonymous or known).
- Same-sex male partners use IUI and a traditional surrogate to carry the child using the sperm of one of the partners.
- Same-sex male partners use IVF and a gestational surrogate to carry the child using the sperm of one of the partners and a donated egg.
- Male and female couple use IUI or IVF with either an egg, sperm, or embryo donor to transfer into the intended mother or into a surrogate.
- Single male uses IUI with the use of his own sperm or donated sperm in a traditional surrogate or uses IVF with a gestational surrogate and an egg donor.
- Single female uses IUI or IVF with a sperm donor.
- Two women in a relationship can undergo simultaneous embryo transfers and carry concurrently with the same due date.
- Two men can combine their sperm for insemination into a surrogate where the source of the genetic material may be unknown unless tested.

Checking Out Your Embryos

Preimplantation genetic diagnosis (PGD) and preimplantation genetic screening (PGS), which is legal in the United States but illegal in certain countries around the world, is performed at some fertility clinics to screen the embryo for inherited diseases. A view from under the microscope, embryologist and IVF laboratory director Dr. Michael B. Matilsky describes these procedures as follows:

PGD provides a couple at risk of having children with a known genetic disease with the possibility of transferring only unaffected embryos, and discarding affected embryos. Typically, only single gene mutation diseases are currently identifiable by biochemical analysis of the embryonic DNA. PGD can detect at least 25 different single gene mutation diseases, including thalassemias, phenylketonuria, cystic fibrosis, Gaucher's disease, Tay-Sachs disease, and fragile X-chromosome syndrome, among others. Although PGD was first introduced in 1990, the technique has undergone several adjustments in methodology and improvements in reliability. Today, the best technologies make use of laser-assisted surgical removal of day 5 or day 6 blastocyst trophectoderm cells. These cells are shipped to a genetic analysis laboratory for processing and diagnosis. The post-surgical embryos are frozen individually by quick freezing (vitrification) to await diagnosis. The genetic report usually takes one to two weeks for final results. At that time, the patient can find out which of their embryos are available for thawing and transfer at a later date. Genetically normal embryos have about a 70 percent chance of promoting a successful pregnancy.

Preimplantation genetic screening has also become popular but has several drawbacks, including its expense and true lack of proven efficacy in increasing pregnancy rates beyond that achievable by transfer of a quantity of two day-5 blastocysts. PGS uses the same surgical techniques as PGD, but limits it analysis of "normal" embryos to the detection of the correct number of pairs of chromosomes (22 autosomes and either XX for girls or XY for boys). Although incorrect number of chromosomes is the major contributor to miscarriages and the most common diagnosis in aborted fetuses, it is not the only cause of implantation failure. Even when genetically normal embryos are transferred, the chance of successful pregnancy does not exceed 70 percent (i.e., this technique does not guarantee success).

FDA Guidelines Both Clarify and Confuse

The FDA has strict guidelines in the manner it regulates ART to ensure the safety of those going through the process. According to Dr. Mark Denker of Palm Beach Fertility (http://www.palmbeachfertility.com), the FDA guidelines regulating third-party reproduction can "clarify and confuse" those in the ART world:

> Recently, third-party reproduction has come under the watch of the FDA through the Current Good Tissue Practice (CGTP) requirements regulating human cells, tissues, and cellular- and tissue-based products. Because sperm and eggs from two parties are utilized and implanted into the uterus of a party that is not a sexually intimate partner of either party donating the sperm or the egg, the FDA requires eggs and sperm be screened to the same level of safety that any tissue would be screened prior to transplantation, such as a heart or lung. It becomes incumbent upon the physicians to ensure the procedure and donated biological tissues are 100 percent safe. In essence, the intended parents are regarded as gamete "donors" in relationship to the surrogate.
>
> The FDA allows some flexibility for couples undergoing gestational surrogacy, since the intended parents know the surrogate. Terminology surrounding this and the regulations mandated by the FDA has given rise to much confusion in practices. The FDA uses the term "ineligible" to describe a donor that tests positive for a disease on its donor-eligibility determination screening list. However, that person is not by default ineligible to donate gametes; he or she may be eligible to donate gametes with an additional FDA waiver, informed consent, and proper labeling.
>
> In a case of positivity of FDA infectious disease screening, the FDA allows a consent and waiver form, acknowledging that there may be a potential risk of transmission of infectious disease. Therefore, the recipient (i.e., the surrogate) has been informed and all parties have accepted the risk. Any gametes (sperm, eggs, or embryos) that are untested or have tested positive must be clearly labeled as such.

All clinics performing assisted reproductive techniques should have policy and procedure manuals addressing how to handle sperm, eggs, or embryos that test positive for various infections agents. Even so, not all clinics accept patients or commissioning couples that test positive on FDA screening tests. Therefore, it is advisable for patients to proactively inquire on a clinic-by-clinic basis to see if there are any reproductive restrictions focused on infectious disease policies. The increased incidence of hepatitis B, hepatitis C, and HIV have created common problems that have yet to be addressed in order to bring this innovative reproductive option to those in need.

Choosing a Fertility Clinic

While it is great to have options in selecting fertility clinics, deciding where to receive medical treatment can be a difficult decision to make due to the numerous clinics available for ART.

Rhonda Levy had her own experience struggling with infertility and is the founder and CEO of Empowered IVF (http://www.empoweredivf.com), a consulting service that helps heterosexual, LGBT couples, and singles throughout the world navigate the world of ART. Levy shares the following guide on selecting a good fertility clinic:

What Characteristics Do High-Quality Fertility Clinics Possess?

Fertility clinics of the highest quality tend to have leaders who have created a culture of excellence. Inside their walls, it is expected that everyone on staff will pay obsessively close attention to detail.

Although some clinics continue to take an outdated approach to IVF, even after it has been eclipsed by new advances, the approach of the most successful fertility clinics is always in step with the most recent scientific advances. In fact, it is often these top-tier fertility clinics that are at the forefront conducting the most important research and making the most significant strides in propelling IVF technology forward.

The best fertility clinics make considerable financial investments in their laboratories to ensure that they are "state-of-the-art," and staff them with some of the world's most highly skilled embryologists and technicians. As a result, when their patients create healthy embryos, these clinics are capable of cultivating them to their maximum potential to implant and become a baby.

High-quality fertility clinics also take an obsessively careful approach beyond the laboratory, on the clinical side of care. Their physicians believe in the importance of conducting an exhaustive patient workup to ensure a proper diagnosis and to identify and address any correctable impediments to the success of the patient's IVF cycle before it begins. They have multiple stimulation protocols and tailor each woman's stimulation to ensure that she will have her best possible yield of eggs. And finally, high-quality fertility clinics take very seriously the importance of conducting a transfer that is free of trauma so that patient's embryo or embryos will have their best possible chance of implanting in the uterus.

Why Is It Important to Learn How to Analyze Fertility Clinic Success Rates?

The best way for patients to assess from the outside whether a fertility clinic possesses a culture of excellence is to analyze its success rates. Only fertility clinics that have success rates significantly above the national average are truly outstanding. Patients should never pursue IVF until after they have conducted an exhaustive comparative analysis of fertility clinic statistics. Not only can a patient's fertility clinic choice make all the difference between whether they will or will not ultimately have a baby but it can also reduce the number of failed IVF cycles they will experience or even eliminate them, together with the financial, physical, and emotional trauma that comes with them.

The SART Registry and the CDC's ART Success Rate Reports:
Tools for Analyzing IVF Outcomes

Online information on IVF outcomes for fertility clinics produced by two distinct entities—the Society for Assisted Reproductive Technology (SART) (http://www.sart.org/find_frm.html) and the Centers for Disease Control (CDC) (http://www.cdc.gov/art/reports/index.html)—are easily accessible to those pursuing IVF in the United States. Their public availability can be an enormous advantage to those navigating what is a highly complex fertility clinic landscape.

SART is the primary organization of professionals dedicated to the practice of ART in the United States. Established in 1986, it began to compile data about IVF outcomes from its member clinics that same year. The SART registry is comprised of a national summary and standardized individual fertility clinic success rate reports.

In 1992, the Federal Trade Commission intervened in a case of false advertising by a fertility clinic. This inspired the US Congress to hold hearings that led to the passage of the Fertility Clinic Success Rate and Certification Act. This legislation, passed in 1992, requires American fertility clinics to collect detailed clinic-specific data on every cycle of ART they perform and to submit it to the CDC, which is then required to make it easily accessible to the public online. The CDC published the first ART Success Rate Report in 1997 based on ART procedures performed in 1995. Like the SART registry, it is also comprised of a national summary and standardized individual fertility clinic success rate reports.

Introduction of a New Reporting Structure

Starting in 2016, patients will be introduced to a new reporting structure for the SART Registry and the CDC's ART Success Rate Report, beginning with treatments that occurred in 2014. The original reporting structure for these registries was developed when the primary focus of IVF was on the transfer of fresh embryos. The new structure was made necessary when the primary focus for many clinics became the transfer of frozen embryos. This shift in focus is the result of a number of factors, including advances made in vitrification (freezing) techniques, the increasing popularity of (PGS), which generally involves the freezing of embryos, and studies that show improved implantation rates and better obstetrical outcomes when embryos are transferred on a normal cycle (not the stimulation cycle).

Understanding the Subtleties and Nuances

The public availability of fertility clinic success rates has always been a double-edged sword. Competition for patients has motivated some clinics to engage in practices that put a positive spin on their success rates to attract market share, such as denying IVF to poor prognosis patients. Despite this, patients seeking treatment in the United States are better off than those in some other countries where no registry exists, and where patients are virtually blindfolded when choosing a fertility clinic.

Because of the recent advances in IVF, fertility clinic success rates have never been more difficult to interpret than they are today. Patients using the SART Registry and the CDC ART Success Rate Report must make a conscious effort to learn how to identify clinics that engage in practices that shine a favorable light on their success rates for their own financial benefit, and about the many other subtleties and nuances that are not immediately apparent on the surface of the reports.

Other Factors to Consider

Once patients narrow their focus to top performing fertility clinics, there are other factors that will enable them to make an intelligent, thoughtful, and fully informed choice. It is generally wise for patients to schedule consultations with more than one clinic. Although patients might expect consistency in the opinions held by strong clinics, they will discover that they often differ quite dramatically in their views and in their approaches to treatment. Patients will benefit if, prior to the consultations, they become informed about how (and why) treatment approaches vary from clinic to clinic. This will allow them to arrive at the consultations armed with penetrating questions that will help them understand each clinic's rationale for their views and to then reconcile them in a meaningful way. Once patients truly understand why each clinic operates as it does, their instincts will help them decide which clinic's culture and approach feels most "right" for them.

Levy's Own Journey to Motherhood via IVF

It was my own struggle to become a mother via IVF that inspired me to become professionally involved in this world. In this piece, originally published in an online magazine for women called *xojane*, I tell the story of the difficult journey that led to the birth of my twin sons in 1996: http://www.xojane.com/healthy/best-ivf-clinics.

CHAPTER

2

Psychological Implications—Wrapping Your Mind around ART

Not only does assisted reproductive technology (ART) have medical, legal, and financial implications, it also raises powerful emotional considerations for intended parents, donors, surrogates, and the families of those involved in ART or those suffering from infertility.

Many people find solace with a mental health professional or support organization when suffering from infertility as the disorder of infertility can create a most distressing life crisis.

Sufferers of infertility may voluntarily seek out the assistance of a therapist or support group to help cope with the physical and emotional challenges associated with infertility. However, intended parents considering third-party reproduction and donors of egg, sperm, or embryos are all recommended to consult with a mental health professional before embarking on a third-party ART procedure. This recommendation is a voluntary guideline established by the American Society for Reproductive Medicine. While these intended parents may not have voluntarily seen a therapist prior to performing the embryo transfer, many find that the session helps sort out their feelings, reduces their anxiety and depression regarding the process, and helps them mentally prepare for the challenges raised by third-party assisted reproduction.

According to the ASRM, the emotions experienced with infertility have been compared to other major life events such as death of a family member or separation and/or divorce.

Emotional Aspects of Infertility

For someone that easily gets pregnant, it's hard to imagine that trying to have a baby is emotionally painful. Stress and anxiety build as medical procedures may not work, costs compound procedure after procedure, work and relationships are strained, and the dream that one may have of how they thought their family would be created continues to change into a more clinical vision. Despair often sets in.

Karyn Rosenberg (http://www.karynrosenberg.com), licensed clinical social worker, who provides fertility counseling and third-party reproduction counseling and consultations, shares her professional insight on the emotional impacts of family building, infertility, and third-party reproduction can cause:

> Becoming a mother or father and having a baby is something many people assume will happen naturally and exactly at the time you are ready to have a family. But for so many people struggling with fertility issues, single parenting by choice, or same-sex parenting makes the journey very lengthy, emotionally difficult, and financially challenging. There are many psychological and emotional impacts that you may face. Many people feel there is something wrong with them. It is very normal to feel a sense of sadness, loss, anxiety, loneliness, and anger. Coping with infertility brings about a sense of grief and loss. It is one of the most difficult challenges that anyone has had to face. It is so important to not blame yourself and let go of the angry and negative voices that are in your head. When you feel this way, it is so important to let go, and truly focus on the present trying to be in the moment as much as possible.
>
> If you have a partner, remember that communication is the key to dealing with the emotional roller coaster ride you and your partner have embarked upon. The only way to understand each other's feelings is through open communication. Listening to one another creates a level of intimacy that can really help, as you remain attentive and present to each other. Learning what you can about the unknown helps you gain control during a time in life that feels out of control. Try to keep a sense of balance in your life. If you work, keep working. If you have a hobby, stay involved in it. It's ok to say no. Don't feel like you have to attend every baby shower you are invited to. You also don't have to tell everyone what you are going through. Create play in your life. Dealing with fertility issues can feel like a full-time job, so it's so important to take time out for movies, music, and other enjoyable activities. A little pampering may be just what the doctor ordered. Indulge in a massage or pedicure. Make sure you are exercising and eating healthily. Finding your inner peace can help you tap into strength you didn't know you had. Many people find prayer or meditation to be helpful. For some people, the crisis you face may make you feel like you can't cope or are "going crazy." You are definitely not alone. These feelings are a normal part of the process and you may need the support of others through a support group or individual counseling to help normalize your experience.

Emotional Aspects of Third-Party Reproduction (Egg, Sperm, Embryo Donation, and Surrogacy)

When considering using a surrogate or egg, sperm, or embryo donor, the American Society for Reproductive Medicine (ASRM) guidelines provide that these decisions are complex; and that patients and their partners may benefit from psychosocial education to aid in these decisions. The fertility physician should strongly recommend counseling by a qualified mental health professional to all intended parents and donor recipients and their partners.

Licensed Psychologist Lauren K. Cohn, Ph.D. (http://www.psychologicalstrategies.com), works with ART patients and has the following guidance on the process of working with a mental health professional when considering third-party reproduction that includes using an egg, sperm, or embryo donor or a surrogate:

The psychological consultation is an essential part of the preparation for treatment. There are several goals of this consultation. The primary reason for the consultation is to ensure that individuals and couples fully understand some of the issues involved in third-party reproduction. Reproductive technology has progressed by leaps and bounds. However, each of these treatments brings unique challenges to the table. Mental health professionals (MHPs) working in this field are trained to help individuals and couples understand these challenges and decide how to best manage them. This aspect of the consultation is considered to be psycho-education, which means educating clients about the psychological aspects of the medical treatment. Some clinics also require that MHPs include an evaluative component in the consultation. The MHP will evaluate all parties involved to ensure that there are no psychological issues that can interfere with successful treatment. This is critical for donors and gestational carriers. Many intended parents worry that they will be prevented from moving ahead with their plan. However, this generally is not the case. Instead, information obtained by the MHP can be used to develop recommendations for the clinic that will help them to provide the best care for intended parents. It will be important to clarify with your MHP whether the goal of your consultation is psycho-education or evaluative.

The specific details of your mental health consultation will depend on the type of treatment that you are pursuing. If you and your partner will be using donor eggs or donor sperm, you will meet with the MHP to discuss various aspects of this treatment. If you are using a donor who is known to you, your donor will undergo a psychological evaluation, and then you will be asked to participate in a session with your donor. The donor's spouse/partner will also be included. The purpose of this joint session is to ensure that everyone understands the implications of a known-donor arrangement. Further, the session will help all parties to clarify expectations for the relationship between the parties, both during treatment and after the child is born. The same is true for individuals and couples using a gestational carrier. The session will include a discussion of potential decisions that may need to be made during pregnancy. When the couples do not agree, the MHP can explore the feelings and beliefs of each participant in order to help them work out an arrangement that satisfies everyone.

When you meet with the MHP, you will be asked questions about your experience with infertility and how you came to the decision to participate in third-party reproduction. The counselor will talk with you and your partner about how you coped with the challenges of infertility and how you manage your feelings about needing to rely on someone else in order to build your family. One challenge experienced by intended parents using ART is that at least one parent will not share a genetic connection to their child. The MHP will talk with you about the loss of this genetic relationship and help you manage your feelings about this.

Treatment decisions will also be addressed in the consultation session. Issues such as the number of embryos to transfer during in vitro fertilization (IVF), feelings about a multiple pregnancy, and how to manage such a pregnancy will be reviewed. One option is to use selective reduction, a procedure in which the doctor medically reduces the number of babies in the pregnancy. The counselor will help you to balance your feelings about the number of embryos to transfer and your feelings about selective reduction. Decisions about the disposition of unused embryos will also be addressed. The MHP will help you to consider these issues in terms of your culture and your religious beliefs.

One of the most important issues covered in the psychological consultation is that of disclosure. Most intended parents struggle with the decision about whether to tell their child that he or she was created with the help of another person. If the intended parents have decided to tell, they are often uncertain about what to say and when to say it. Your MHP can help you to explore your feelings about disclosure and help you to arrive at a decision that makes sense for you.

If you are using a known donor or a gestational carrier, the joint meeting is a critically important piece of the process. When using a known donor, the MHP will help all parties clarify expectations for the donor's future role with the child. For example, will your known egg donor be a "special auntie" or do the intended parents prefer to limit contact and try to forget about the fact that they needed a donor? Does the donor feel the same way?

When using a gestational carrier, the issues are more complex. The first consideration is whether the carrier and her partner want the same type of relationship as do the intended parents. This is pertinent both during the pregnancy and as the child grows up. Important decisions include the frequency of contact between the intended parent and the gestational carrier and who will be present at medical appointments and at the delivery. Will the families continue the relationship after the child's birth or will the intended parents agree only to send a picture on an annual basis? It is also important to consider issues in pregnancy management. These issues include the number of embryos to transfer, decisions about selective reduction, the use of prenatal testing, and pregnancy termination in the event that there is a problem with the fetus. In addition, the intended parents and the carrier need to come to some decisions about lifestyle choices such as diet, activities, and travel during the pregnancy.

How to Find a Mental Health Professional with ART Experience

Like any of the players in an ART journey, it is important to pick professionals that are experienced specifically with ART-related matters. Someone with years of experience as a "family lawyer" does not necessarily have experience in and knowledge of the finer details of ART. In addition to the required counseling associated with surrogacy or egg, sperm, or embryo donation, someone going through ART procedures should independently consider seeking counseling if they are feeling depressed, anxious, or so consumed by the fertility process that it is difficult to function in society.

According to the ASRM, in selecting a mental health professional, it is recommended to interview more than one person, ask them for their credentials as well as their experience with infertility issues and treatments, and make sure the therapist has:

According to the ASRM, some signs that one may need counseling to guide you through the challenges of ART include social isolation, mood swings, difficulty with scheduled intercourse constant preoccupation with infertility marital problems, just to name a few impacts seen with ART challenges.

- a graduate degree in a mental health profession
- a license to practice and/or state registration
- clinical training in the psychological aspects of infertility
- experience in the medical and psychological aspects of reproductive medicine

Birds and the Bees: How to Talk to Children of ART

While it is certainly the choice of the intended parents to inform their child that they were conceived through IVF, an egg/sperm donor, and/or through a surrogate, in line with proponents of disclosure, as often disclosed in the same context as adoption, it is strongly recommended based on the available research that the method of conception be disclosed to a child and is in the best interest of the child born through ART.

Licensed clinical social worker, Karyn Rosenberg, emphasizes the importance of considering how to talk to children born as a result of ART:

As if having the "birds and the bees" talk about where babies come from isn't awkward enough for parents and children, having to discuss how babies are created with ART may involve a little more medical detail.

Considering how to talk with children about how they were conceived is something all intended parents need to consider. It is important to think about honesty and respect, and the challenge of keeping secrets. If the decision was made to tell the child, sharing this at an early age in an organic and natural way while being age appropriate helps the child begin to understand the concepts, and assists with reducing anxieties by the parent. Using books and illustrations for children help to navigate the conversations in a very helpful way. Sometimes it is not always the details about conception, but the communication with the child that can bring about the most important part of relationship between parent and child.

How to Help a Friend Struggling with ART Challenges

Infertility is a disease. Foot-in-the-mouth is also an ailment that friends and family need to be mindful of when talking to those struggling with infertility. Someone going through infertility can be extremely sensitive to even innocuous comments, even as simple as telling them to relax. It is important to be mindful of what you say when speaking to someone you know who is going through ART procedures.

There are many things *not* to say to someone experiencing infertility (i.e., complaining or bragging about your pregnancy or telling them there are worse things that could happen to them). Yet it is challenging to know what to say to someone going through this process and does require consideration.

Let's face it; some people are more sensitive than others. However, isn't it better to be safe than sorry? Infertility advocate and former ART patient Marisa Horowitz-Jaffe compiled a list of things to say to someone experiencing infertility that is collected from her own experience and from other women who have also suffered with infertility.

1. "I don't know exactly what you are experiencing, but I'm here to listen and support you in whatever way I can."
2. "How can I be a better friend to you during this time?"
3. I really wish people would have acknowledged the difficulty of the process rather than simply glossing over it. For example, it would have been nice to hear: "I know this is a tough situation/process/time and I am here for you." Something simple and not too dramatic, but heartfelt, nonetheless.
4. I would have liked to have been asked about the treatment/process without the listener becoming incredulous about how much I had to endure and how "they could never have done it." Basically, just listening would have been good.
5. Sometimes there isn't anything you can say that won't offend or hurt someone going through infertility especially if the person is pregnant or has children. Sometimes you just have to listen.

ART and Lifestyle Choices

Just relax and you will get pregnant. It's probably one of the most irritating things someone can say to a person experiencing infertility or struggling with building a family. As time passes, pregnancy is still not yet achieved, the medical bills increase, and the stress of the process builds and compounds on a person. While it is hard to prove that stress impacts infertility, it is believed that reducing stress provides a better quality of life during times of intense personal challenge. So, while running on the elliptical machine for hours may not get you pregnant, the act of exercise may just make you feel better about yourself and have a clean mind during the ART process.

Beyond managing stress, it is recommended that those going through ART should focus on the effects of their professional environment and overall quality of life. Take into consideration sources of stress and monitor your diet, which includes the consumption of too much caffeine, smoking, drugs, and alcohol. Aim to maintain a healthy weight and consider the time spent using electronic devices.

Those experiencing fertility challenges should focus on reducing these negative factors in their lives and thus improving their quality of life in conjunction with ART.

Acupuncture for ART

Going through fertility treatments is akin to being like pin cushions—constantly being poked and prodded by different needles and medical devices. To add to the poking and prodding, but in a relaxing manner, many fertility doctors recommend that patients and surrogates utilize acupuncture to increase fertility success and reduce stress. Coauthor Marla B. Neufeld utilized and enjoyed acupuncture, coupled with Chinese herbs (approved by her physician), to assist with her reproductive efforts.

Board-certified acupuncturist in Diplomat of Oriental Medicine, Dr. Michael Fiorani of Plantation Acupuncture (http://www.PlantationAcupuncture.org) highlights four major ways acupuncture can improve implantation rates, pregnancy rates, and live birth rates based on empirical evidence and published scientific studies:

1. Regulating menstrual cycle through its influence on the hypothalamus-pituitary-gonadal (HPG) and adrenal (HPA) axes. One of the most important functions of the HPG axis is to regulate reproduction by controlling the uterine and ovarian cycles, which may be the most important key to acupuncture and fertility.
2. Regulating uterine and ovarian blood flow, which can thicken the endometrium and enhance receptivity for implantation.
3. Impact on T-helper cytokines. Recurrent implantation failure and miscarriages have been linked in several studies to increased TH-1 cytokine expressions. Studies have proposed that acupuncture, through its ability to increase the release of β-endorphin, may improve the poor receptive state of the endometrium and implantation by promoting TH-2 cytokines secretion and inhibiting TH-1 cytokines.
4. Treating stress, depression, and anxiety. Because infertility can cause stress, which leads to a release of stress hormones, it has been suggested that stress reduction might improve fertility. Simply put, there are various studies that show that groups of women with higher stress, depression, anxiety, and negative emotions are associated with lower pregnancy rates. Studies have also shown a beneficial regulation of cortisol and prolactin levels in acupuncture groups during the medication phase of the IVF treatment.

A Personal Story of Struggle with ART

A Christian perspective on ART—Psalm 113:9—He gives the barren woman a home, making her the joyous mother of children. Praise the LORD!

Ryan Hall is an inspiring pastor in Jacksonville, Florida. He and his wife, Jessamyn, are the parents to beautiful twin girls named Evelyn and Jenna that were presented to them through surrogacy. Ryan shares a Christian perspective on ART and his experience with surrogacy:

The anguished sobs were ripping apart the voice on the phone and tearing me to pieces as well. I can never forget the sound of my wife's voice fighting to put words to the unspeakable. Cancer. How could it be cancer? How does a young, vibrant woman with a heart on fire get cancer? God had given us a heart to be parents, and uterine cancer necessitating a hysterectomy was shutting all that down. I can never forget that call, that shockwave of shattered dreams.

I did not know just how angry and scared I really was until I walked back to the surgical waiting room when they took Jessamyn away to cut into her. Family sat with me while I withdrew into myself and tried to mask my terror with jokes. I could barely pray. Thankfully the surgery went well and was over in only a few hours, and Jessamyn was discharged the very next day. Her recovery was painful and required a lot of care. This afforded us time to strengthen our faith. It was a time to not only get better but to get ready.

After Jessamyn was able to walk without pain, her focus immediately returned to that dim but tantalizing hope of having children. The oncologist allowed a twelve-month window before the ovaries would have to come out, but this would hopefully give us a chance to boost Jessamyn's normal egg production and perhaps allow us to have children using another woman's womb. All we needed was to find someone who would take the risk with us and allow us the use of her womb. How exactly does a couple procure a willing womb? This was when surrogacy shifted from a plot line in TV dramas to a lifeline for all our hopes.

In the materials from the clinic, we located a single number for a surrogacy agency. We called the number, met with the agency's representatives, and about seven weeks later we were sitting in a coffee shop ready to meet Joanna. She had already passed all the necessary criteria, and that day, Jessamyn tearfully asked her to be our surrogate. Through her own tears, Joanna said yes! We were elated! From a deep darkness of doubt and frustration to suddenly having a beautiful soul willing to take a chance with us, we were overwhelmed with joy!

Almost immediately, some doubt began to creep in. Through all of this, we had focused on our own grief, fear, and hope. We had prayed and prayed, but most of our prayers were basically pleas for some sort of breakthrough mixed with appeals for comfort. We knew we desperately wanted children and that this was the only visible chance, but was this right? As we negotiated the contracts and learned about all the procedures we also wondered, is God okay with this? Were we about to play at being God?

The Bible has several stories where women who seemed barren were blessed with miracle children. Sarah was ninety when God promised she would have a son. She was so incredulous that she laughed. About nine months later she named her newborn son "Isaac," meaning "laughter" (Genesis 18). In another story, a barren wife, Hannah, pray[s] desperately in the temple for God to open her womb. She promised that if God would but give her a son, she would dedicate him to the Lord's service. Her petitions were so passionate the priest at first thought she was drunk. Just a few years later, she presented her boy, Samuel, to that very same priest (1 Samuel 1–2). Elizabeth is another older woman who was barren when the angel Gabriel announced that she was about to become the mother of John the Baptist (Luke 1).

Jesus' own origins are anything but conventional. Mary was engaged to be married when she was found to be pregnant. Everybody knows where babies come from, who would ever believe she was virgin? She was a shameful woman. Joseph was instructed by God in a dream about the truth, but still, everyone in their village still thought they knew exactly what happened. Perhaps Mary was a loose woman. Perhaps Joseph just could not wait to bed her down. Either way, they were probably viewed as the worst sort of people. Looking further back we see Jesus' family tree populated with more of these worst sorts of people. We find murderers, swindlers, idolaters, womanizers, at least one rapist, and two prostitutes (Matthew 1). It is not clean and neat. It indicates that God is so committed to our redemption—our rescue from the very worst that we can become—that God will respond to our regrettable, and even our despicable acts, with grace.

As we kept moving ahead, we leaned into that grace. If we were making a mistake, we could still trust in God's grace. As we kept reflecting we also considered the blessing of human ingenuity and the benefits of science. God created us with our tremendous capacity and drive to explore our world and probe the depths of the mysteries of creation. Much of the science that is contained in the Bible seems so antiquated and preposterous that we do not recognize it. Jacob attempted genetic modification in sheep to cheat his uncle Laban using shaved sticks. We know they had no effect whatsoever, but he thought they did. Some of the instructions and stories regarding skin diseases, demon possession, and miracle healings involve ancient medicinal practices that seem laughable or ridiculous. And yet healing happened. Could it be that God encourages and even blesses scientific exploration and advancement?

Jacob, the father of the twelve tribes of Israel, was blessed with thirteen children because his two wives, Leah and Rachel, were sisters locked in a competition to produce offspring. The battle of the babies includes one particular scene involving primitive medicine. Leah and Rachel made a deal where Rachel would get to use some mandrakes, plants that were believed to bolster sexual arousal and fertility, but in this case they did not work. It was Leah who got pregnant, again (Genesis 30:14–17). Here we see the science of humanity as limited and ineffective. We still see this today. Sometimes treatments work, and sometimes they do not.

Once all the papers were signed and the green light was given, we began the process and were immediately swept up in it. We had never before been so disciplined as we managed multiple shots and scans and precise timing. When we got to extraction day, we were told to expect six to eight eggs. Jessamyn had produced twenty-five. In the next few days we learned that of those twenty-five eggs, fifteen had been fertilized. We were stunned and confused. Why so many? What are the implications for the sanctity of life? We only had two embryos survive, but we still wonder about those others. Were they properly alive? We never landed in a solid place with that one. Every year on All Saints Sunday our church has a service to honor and remember the family members we have lost. We place thirteen little blooms before the Communion Table and pray God's peace and presence for our lost embryos. There are some things neither faith nor science fully discloses. Laying the flowers helps.

As the miracle pregnancy progressed, we got to know Joanna in the shared awkwardness of the forced vulnerability of the frequent prenatal checks. We also began to meet for monthly meals, and Jessamyn and Joanna kept in close contact. We considered from the beginning that we would much prefer to keep our gestational carrier in our lives for the psychosocial health of the children, and Joanna made that decision so much easier. We knew so little about each other, but our mutual commitment to bring life into the world in the best way we could knitted our hearts together in a very deep way. She was a willing participant in the shared hope of bringing new life into the world. We were partners. She became family. As God was weaving together the bodies of our children in Joanna's womb, God was weaving our hearts together into a family unit. We did not just gain two children through this arrangement. We gained Aunt Joanna, her daughter, and now her fiancé and his children. The love of God has expanded in us and around us beyond our wildest expectations.

Our story and the powerful bonds we have forged with Aunt Joanna and our expanded family have given the girls a powerful origin story. They are miracles. Our story is right in line with the miracle births of the Bible, and in fact all the births of every human being. Considering the odds, we are all miracle children. Each one of us, not just our twin daughters, is a living testament to this true fact: God will stop at nothing to bring love into the world. No amount of hatred, brutality, or evil of any kind, will hamper God's work of redeeming life with life.

God is the source of everything good in the world, including the goodness that can be found in human beings, God's rebellious offspring. We have received the children we could barely hope for. We also received an expanded family. We have experienced waves of loving support in our grief and in our joy. We are raising our children with a sure sense of dedication. These are the Lord's girls. They are living witnesses to God's extravagant love and incomprehensible generosity. They are living witnesses of the power of God bringing strangers together and uniting them as a family. They are love alive and let loose in the world.

Sometime in the future, perhaps at their high school graduation or at their weddings, there is going to be an opportunity to contrast their beautifully mature, young adult pictures with their baby pictures. We have no shortage of footage to choose from, but I already know exactly the picture I want. It is a grainy, black and white, micrograph of the girls when they were blastocysts. Just about sixteen cells each. It seems a rare gift to have a picture of the interweaving of science, faith, hope, and love. What a wonder to be alive, and what a delight to share life together. This is God's good gift to all of us.

CHAPTER

3

Financial Implications of ART

Show Me the Money—Expenses Relating to ART

It's hard for anyone in the depths of assisted reproductive technology (ART) procedures to believe that having a child can actually be free for some people! A wide range of techniques are offered for ART procedures and with that comes a range of fees for the medical procedures involved. Examples of variables that impact the cost depend on if an egg or sperm donor is required, if the cycle is a fresh IVF cycle or frozen IVF cycle, the medication protocol, and if there are any medical complications that arise during the process. The location where the ART procedures take place impacts fees as they vary depending on the city, state, or country. Studies show that in areas with fewer infertility clinics, the costs are actually higher for treatment; an area with a higher cost of living does not necessarily equate to higher ART costs.

Costs of Common ART Procedures

It is difficult to find an average for fees of ART procedures as many fertility clinics charge different amounts; most clinics do not publish the treatment rates or payment terms on their website. Patients should have a consultation with the clinic's financial staff to formulate a budget and payment plan for the medical expenses.

Questions to Ask Fertility Clinics Relating to Costs

It is challenging to know what questions to ask a fertility clinic when you are new to the infertility world and don't know the intricacies of ART finances. It is recommended that patients considering ART do their due diligence in the beginning and have a meeting with the fertility clinic's financial department to have a detailed conversation about the costs involved, payment plans and financial assistance options. Some questions to guide you in talking to the financial department include:

1. Does the clinic have a detailed list of procedures and corresponding costs? This list should include the common ART procedures like IVF and IUI, medical procedures associated with standard screening of new patients, and should also include additional procedures that may be necessary such as ICSI, PGD, storage fees for frozen embryos, etc.
2. Are medications, tests, lab work, ultrasounds, and consultations included in the cost of treatment?
3. If necessary, what are the costs, including screening costs, involved when using an egg donor, sperm donor, or surrogate?
4. What are the typical costs associated with medications?
5. Does the fertility clinic provide financial counseling and psychological counseling? If so, are there fees for these services?
6. Does my medical insurance cover any of the medications, testing, monitoring, or procedures and does the fertility clinic verify coverage or is that the patient's responsibility?
7. When is payment due? Is payment required upfront? Is a payment plan available?
8. Does the fertility clinic offer a reduced rate if you purchase an IVF package?

Surrogacy Costs

The expenses in surrogacy are multifaceted. Not only do you have to consider the costs associated with the ART medical procedures described above but you also have to factor in other expenses such as the "compensation" and/or "payments" to a surrogate, among other expenses.

When doing your research on budgets, keep in mind that every state has different standards for costs associated with the process. For example, some states prohibit "compensation" to the surrogate. In these states, the concept of "altruistic surrogacy," wherein the surrogate does not get paid a fee for her services, benefits the intended parents in that they can only pay the surrogate's out-of-pocket expenses and medical expenses. However, surrogates looking to be compensated for their efforts will

Part of ART is mastering the "art" of formulating a budget for each procedure taking place.

look outside such states, which can thus be a detriment for families in the prohibitive state trying to find a good surrogate match. It's a "Catch-22."

Compensation and Payments to the Surrogate

The notion of "compensation" and "payment" versus "reimbursement" to a surrogate is somewhat controversial. The language used *may* carry importance insofar as whether the financial portion of the arrangement could or should be considered "income" to the surrogate for taxation purposes.

A surrogacy contract sets out the financial responsibility, however it may be framed, and creates a payment plan that the intended parents will pay their surrogate. When working with a surrogacy agency, the agency establishes the payments made to the surrogate and there is little to no negotiation between the intended parents and surrogate as to what she will be receiving financially. When self-matching occurs and no agency is involved, the parties, either directly or through the lawyers, negotiate the payment terms to a surrogate. When using a surrogate, with an agency or self-matched, the amounts paid to a surrogate will be different depending on where the surrogacy is taking place.

A surrogacy budget can be broken down into three categories: (i) payments the surrogate should receive, (ii) payments the surrogate may receive depending on whether certain events occur, and (iii) payments to third parties involved in the process.

Payments the Surrogate Should Receive

As seen in most surrogacy contracts, from the moment a surrogate is selected until a determined time after the child is born, intended parents can be "on the hook" for payments to a surrogate for weeks or months post birth (depending on the contract). Below are the common payments made to a surrogate:

- **Surrogate's compensation**—Again, care must be paid to use of terms such as "compensation," "payment," "fee," and the like. With that said, this is her "base fee" that typically begins once she is confirmed to be pregnant and continues to receive financial support every four (4) weeks thereafter until the child is born. Many surrogacy contracts require the surrogate to reach a certain week of pregnancy in order for her to receive her entire agreed amount (for example, thirty weeks, gestation for multiples, thirty-two weeks, gestation for a single child), and if she delivers prior to that determined week, then her compensation would be paid up to that point. A surrogate who has already successfully completed at least one surrogacy will typically be able to receive a higher amount of support than a first-timer.
- **Life insurance and disability insurance policy for the surrogate**—The intended parents are usually required to take out a term life insurance policy and sometimes a disability insurance policy for the surrogate naming someone in the surrogate's family as the beneficiary in case something happens to her during the pregnancy.

- **Medication start**—The surrogate receives a payment at the start of her injectable hormone medications or other type of medication (not including birth control) to prepare her uterus for the embryo transfer.
- **Mock cycle**—Surrogate may receive a payment should the fertility clinic perform a mock embryo cycle, which is essentially a dry run of preparing the surrogate's body for the real embryo transfer.
- **Embryo transfer**—The surrogate receives a payment on the day of the embryo transfer.
- **Monthly allowance**—To cover the surrogate's daily expenses for the pregnancy such as prenatal vitamins, local gas expenses, and groceries, the intended parents may choose to pay the surrogate a monthly allowance instead of the surrogate having to itemize and account for the incidental expenses.
- **Maternity clothes**—The intended parents pay the surrogate an allowance for maternity clothes. The maternity clothing allowance should be higher if the surrogate is carrying twins.
- **Surrogate's travel**—Some surrogates live close to a fertility clinic and hospital, but some may live in different cities, states, or countries than the intended parents. In such cases, the intended parents are required to pay for the surrogate's (and sometimes the surrogate's partner or spouse) out-of-pocket travel expenses for all procedures involved including the initial screening, monitoring, embryo transfer, doctor appointments, and delivery of the child. The travel expenses may include gas, car rental, taxi, hotels, airfare, trains, and a per diem amount if the travel requires an overnight stay.

Typical Payments the Surrogate May Receive

- **Loss of reproductive organs**—Pregnancy is risky; surrogates are compensated should something happen to any of her reproductive organs during the course of the pregnancy. There is a monetary value associated with the loss of the surrogate's fallopian tubes, ovaries, or uterus.
- **Embryo transfer cancellation fee**—Some surrogates receive a flat fee if the medications begin but the embryo transfer is cancelled whereby such cancellation is not a result of the surrogate's intentional actions.
- **Selective reduction or elective termination**—Should a selective reduction or elective termination of the pregnancy occur that is permissible under the contract (i.e., the surrogate did not do these procedures against the wishes of the intended parents), the surrogate receives a fee for having to undergo such procedures.
- **Invasive procedures**—An invasive procedure resulting in a payment to the surrogate will include any procedure relating to the pregnancy requiring administration of IV fluids or an overnight stay at the hospital, with the exception of the birth of any child, such as amniocentesis. Invasive procedures should not include any standard procedures relating to the fertility treatments.

- **Ectopic pregnancy**—Should an ectopic pregnancy occur, the surrogate is compensated.
- **Miscarriage**—Should a miscarriage occur, the surrogate is compensated.
- **Cesarean section**—Should the surrogate require a C-section, the surrogate is compensated.
- **Multiples**—If the surrogate is carrying twins or multiples, she receives additional payments for each fetus.
- **Bed rest**—If the surrogate is placed on physician-ordered bed rest (cannot be self-initiated), the surrogate receives her verifiable lost wages for the days she misses work. Some contracts pay surrogates her net lost wages while others pay gross lost wages. If a surrogate has a short-term disability (STD) policy, the intended parents will only be responsible for the lost wages that are not covered by the STD policy. The contract should establish how long the intended parents need to pay the surrogate's lost wages once the child is born. Additionally, some contracts require the intended parents to pay limited lost wages to the surrogate's partner or spouse for the days they accompany her to certain medical appointments or the delivery of the child.
- **Childcare and housekeeping**—The intended parents may be responsible to pay for the surrogate's reasonable childcare and housekeeping expenses during the pregnancy (this may be covered by the monthly allowance), delivery, postdelivery recovery, and if the surrogate is placed on physician-ordered bed rest.
- **Breast milk pumping**—Should the surrogate agree to pump breast milk postbirth, the intended parents should pay either a weekly or monthly fee to the surrogate along with any expenses associated with pumping, such as equipment, milk bags, and shipping. It is important to discuss the parties' rights and responsibilities insofar as the delivery of the breast milk is concerned. If the milk does not arrive at the parents' home in usable condition, does the surrogate have to forego her payment for that period's pumping? We believe that the responsibility should be on the parents to ensure (pun) that the milk arrives in useable condition.
- **Spoiling your surrogate**—In an expression of gratitude towards a surrogate, many intended parents voluntarily spoil their surrogate with tokens of their appreciation such as buying them food, prenatal massages, and gifts for the surrogate and her family. Before you undertake any course of action that is not contemplated in the contract, however, you should check with your attorney to make sure that what you're planning to do is legal in your jurisdiction!

Payments to Third Parties Involved in the Surrogacy Process

- **Fertility doctors**—The intended parents are required to pay any expenses associated with the fertility clinic for the surrogate and intended parents, which includes the screening of the surrogate, including FDA screening, consultations, medications, the embryo transfer, monitoring, blood work, and ultrasounds.

- **Obstetrician**—The intended parents are required to pay any expenses associated with the obstetrician for the surrogate and whatever is not covered by the health insurance of the surrogate.

- **Hospital**—The intended parents are required to pay any expenses associated with the hospital for labor and delivery, including the hospital stay for the surrogate and any complications relating to the surrogate and whatever is not covered by the health insurance of the surrogate. The surrogacy contract should provide how long the intended parents are responsible to pay for the medical expenses of the surrogate once the child is born. Note that the hospital bills associated with the resulting child are charged to the insurance of the intended parents, not the surrogate's insurance.

- **Medical insurance review**—If the intended parents have the medical insurance of the surrogate reviewed by a professional to determine if any exclusion for surrogacy applies, they are responsible for any fees associated with this service.

- **ART lawyers**—The intended parents are responsible to pay their attorney to draft the surrogacy contract and handle the court proceedings necessary to finalize their parental rights of the child. The intended parents also pay for a separate attorney to represent the surrogate. Other legal costs associated with this process may include court filing fees and certified copies.

- **Trusts and estates lawyers**—It is recommended that the intended parents get their estate plan in order to prepare for the child and are responsible to pay for an attorney to draft any necessary wills, trusts, or other estate documents.

- **Immigration lawyer**—When going abroad to use a surrogate or if the intended parents are from another country, an immigration lawyer is involved to ensure the proper citizenship of the child at the expense of the intended parents.

- **Escrow company**—The intended parents pay for the escrow services to administer the payments to the surrogate throughout the surrogacy process.

- **Background information of surrogate**—Usually these expenses are built into the agency costs, but intended parents may need to pay for a criminal background check, home study, or other investigative research on a surrogate.

- **Surrogacy agency**—If the intended parents require a surrogacy agency, they are required to pay the agency fee.

- **Egg donor agency**—If the intended parents require an egg donor agency, they are required to pay the agency fee.

- **Sperm bank**—If the intended parents require a sperm donor, they are required to pay the sperm bank fee or fee to the sperm donor directly.

- **Psychologist**—The intended parents pay for the psychological screening that is required when using a surrogate.
- **Nutritionist**—If the surrogate requires the assistance of a nutritionist, it is at the expenses of the intended parents.
- **Acupuncturist**—If the surrogate requires the assistance of an acupuncturist, it is at the expense of the intended parents.
- **Embryo storage facility**—If the intended parents have frozen viable embryos, should they want to continue freezing the embryos for a length of time, they are required to pay storage facility fees.
- **Courier fee**—If the intended parents want to have a professional transport the frozen embryos from one fertility clinic to another the fertility clinic (i.e., if the donor is in another location from where the embryo transfer occurs), they are required to pay for the proper transportation of the frozen genetic material.

CAUTION

Do you see a theme here? EVERYTHING is at the expense or at least the responsibility of the intended parent(s). The surrogate is responsible for NOTHING. Yes, hopeful parents, it's expensive, and the entire burden of such expense is put on *you.*

Egg Donation Costs

The term *donor* is really a misnomer as egg "donors" are not generally donating their genetic material without being compensated. Leading ART organizations and ART professionals agree that donors of genetic material should be paid for their time, effort and inconvenience, and that the compensation received is not based according to the planned use of the eggs, the number or quality of eggs retrieved, the number or outcome of prior donation cycles, or the donor's ethnic or other personal characteristics. The costs associated with egg donation can be separated into two main categories: (i) payments to the egg donor, and (ii) payments to third parties involved in the egg-donation process.

Payments to the Egg Donor

- **Egg Donor Fee**—The egg donor receives compensation for providing her eggs. Such fee is commonly paid in two installments. One payment is required upon the start of injectable medications for the egg donor and the second is required upon the retrieval of the eggs (regardless if any eggs are retrieved and/or the quality of the eggs, unless it was the intentional fault of the egg donor). While compensation to egg donors varies, the American Society for Reproductive Medicine (ASRM) provides guidelines on compensation to donors in that total payments to donors in excess of $5,000 require justification and sums above $10,000 are not appropriate. In addition to limiting compensation, the nonbinding guidelines forbid paying additional money to egg donors for specific traits such as academic history, physical characterizes, or prior success as a donor.

- **Complications Insurance Plan for the Egg Donor**—Intended parents may be required to purchase a complications policy for the egg donor to cover any major complications that may arise during the medical procedures for the egg donor.
- **Travel for the Egg Donor**—The intended parents will pay for out of pocket travel expenses for the egg donor (and sometimes her partner or spouse) to attend any fertility doctor appointments such as the screening, monitoring, and egg retrieval. The intended parents may be required to pay any verifiable lost wages for the donor if she misses work because of the procedures.

Payments to Third Parties Involved in the Egg Donation

- **Fertility Doctors**—The intended parents are required to pay any expenses associated with the fertility clinic for the egg donor, which includes the screening of the donor, including FDA and genetic screening, consultations, medications, monitoring, blood work and ultrasounds, and the egg retrieval.
- **ART Lawyers**—If the fertility clinic or egg donation program does not provide the proper legal documentation, the intended parents pay for their attorney to draft the egg donor contract. The intended parents also pay for a separate attorney to represent the egg donor.
- **Background Information of Egg Donor**—Usually these expenses are built into the egg agency costs, but intended parents may need to pay for investigative research on an egg donor.
- **Egg Donor Agency**—If the intended parents require an egg donor agency, they are required to pay the agency fee. Many fertility clinics provide a database of fresh and sometimes frozen eggs; there are also frozen egg banks available to intended parents. Some egg donor clinics and providers offer shared egg donor cycles where multiple intended parents share in the eggs retrieved from one donor; this may reduce the expense of the eggs for the intended parents.
- **Psychologist**—The intended parents pay for psychological screening that is required when using an egg donor.
- **Frozen Egg Storage Facility**—If the intended parents have frozen eggs, should they want to continue freezing the eggs for a length of time, they are required to pay storage facility fees.
- **Courier Fee**—If the intended parents want to have a professional transport the frozen egg from one fertility clinic to another the fertility clinic (i.e., if the donor is in another location from where the embryo transfer occurs), they pay for the proper transportation of the frozen genetic material.

Sperm Donation Costs

Sperm donation may be the least expensive piece of the ART pie when compared to egg donation or using a surrogate. Sperm can be obtained from a known donor or through the use of a frozen sperm bank where the donors are usually anonymous. The costs associated with sperm donation can be separated into two main categories: (i) payments to the sperm donor, and (ii) payments to third parties involved in the sperm donation process.

Payments to the Sperm Donor

- **Sperm Donor Fee**—When a man donates his sperm to a sperm bank, he receives a fee typically *per* donated specimen, depending on various factors such as the quality of the sperm provided. This fee is typically not paid to the donor directly by the intended parents as they pay a separate fee to the sperm bank to purchase the sperm. If intended parents are obtaining sperm from a known donor, they may negotiate their own fee for the sperm directly with the donor.

Payments to Third Parties Involved in the Sperm Donation Process

- **Fertility Doctors**—If the intended parents are not getting sperm from a sperm bank or require the assistance of a fertility clinic to screen a sperm donor, the intended parents are required to pay any expenses associated with the fertility clinic for the sperm donor, which includes screening the sperm donor, including the Food and Drug Administration and genetic screening, medications (if any), and consultations.
- **ART Lawyers**—Typically a sperm bank provides the documentation for the sperm donor to sign off on and to relinquish any paternal rights to the donated sperm. However, as seen when using a known sperm donor (like family or a friend), it is imperative that the parties use an ART lawyer to draft the appropriate sperm donation contract. The intended parents also pay for a separate attorney to represent the sperm donor.
- **Background Information of Sperm Donor**—Usually these expenses are built into the sperm bank's costs, but intended parents may need to pay for investigative research on a sperm donor. Some sperm banks charge extra for an additional child or for adult photographs of the donor, other images or videos of the donor, and handwriting analyses of the donors.
- **Sperm Bank**—If the intended parents require a sperm bank, they are required to pay the clinic's fee to purchase the sperm. The cost for the sperm depends on factors such as whether the sperm is washed or not, if it is from an anonymous source, and if specifics regarding the background of the donor—such as whether he has a graduate degree, etc.—are requested.

- **Psychologist**—The intended parents are strongly recommended to participate in psychological counseling, at their expense, when considering the use of donated sperm.
- **Frozen Sperm Storage Facility**—If the intended parents have frozen sperm and want to continue freezing the sperm for a length of time, they can expect to pay storage facility fees.
- **Courier Fee**—If the intended parents want to have a professional transport the frozen sperm to the fertility clinic or home, they are responsible for paying for the proper transportation of the frozen genetic material.

Estimated Expenses for Surrogacy and Egg Donation

As you see, there are variables that come into play when trying to determine the costs of ART procedures. This only gets more complicated as you add on additional services such as surrogacy and egg donation.

Men Having Babies, Inc. (MHB) (http://www.menhavingbabies.org) is a nonprofit organization that provides invaluable services such as educational and practical information to assist gay prospective parents achieve biological parenting, provide consumer feedback on reviews of fertility clinics, and promote the affordability of surrogacy-related services for gay men through financial assistance and the encouragement of transparency and customer feedback.

In order to help all people going through surrogacy and egg donation, MHB developed a Surrogacy Budgeting System. The goal was to decipher and harmonize the divergent cost structures involved in the entire surrogacy and egg donation procedure and develop a generic budget, as of 2015, with expected cost ranges per line item involved in the process.

The charts formulated by MHB pools data gathered from fourteen fertility clinics and sixteen surrogacy and egg donation agencies across the country. MHB continues to update these tables and asks that clinics and agencies provide current pricing sheets at least once a year.

While MHB does not publicize each provider's cost sheet, the broad spectrum of data is used to create a generic budget. The comprehensive listing of all cost components in standardized categories is the first of its kind and provides prospective parents a definitive checklist of all possible costs. While many providers do not offer clear or full estimates to all possible cost components, MHB filled the omissions with data from independent experts and from their experience with the couples that have gone through the organization's assistance program.

The budget is presented in two tables: one has all the nonmedical costs associated with the surrogate: agency and legal costs, compensation, and expenses. The other table has the egg donation and IVF costs: donor matching, legal fees, compensation, and expenses; and medical screening of all parties, IVF treatment, lab fees, medications, monitoring, and other related costs.

Each table includes three columns: minimum estimated expenses, maximum estimated expenses, and the likely cost for each line item on the budget. Note that providers vary considerably in how they define, organize, and price various services. For instance, while most surrogacy agencies quote an "agency/retainer fee," they vary in how inclusive that fee is. For some, it would include all the re-cruiting, screening, legal, and support functions associated with surrogacy. Others will quote separate fees for some of the items, even if they are not optional or provided by third parties.

In the table, Men Having Babies has listed all of the potential components of each general function or service and provided the minimum and maximum costs Men Having Babies has seen associated with these components when they are quoted separately. However in the "Likely cost" column Men Having Babies has only listed the costs associated with the components that are likely to be item-ized, and assumed all the other components should be included in the general agency fee.

The tables include estimated totals per stage or general grouping, such as medical screening or IVF treatment, which are shaded in gray. Each page is also totaled, and these numbers are highlighted in yellow. When considering these numbers, please keep in mind the following notes:

- The totals of each category represent averages of the respective totals across the various providers, but are not always the arithmetic sum of all the itemized components (since not all of these items are necessary or quoted separately).
- To arrive at cost estimates of the entire surrogacy and egg donation, you will need to add up the total of both tables. Currently that would amount to a minimum of $83,000, a likely cost of $122,000, and a typical $191,000 for the high end of the spectrum.
- These totals include only a basic journey—namely they do not include costs associated with having twins, optional medical procedures (such as preimplantation genetic screening), or when more than one IVF cycle is needed (which is the case in about 30 percent of the times). The tables can allow you to calculated likely costs for these scenarios and others, and factor them in based on your circumstances and level of risk aversion.
- While these tables were created by compiling the most up-to-date data from clinics and agencies around the United States, they are only offered as a budgeting aid. Anyone embarking upon a surrogacy and egg donation journey needs to formulate their own budget based on the specific services required and the actual providers being utilized.

In order to better understand the MHB tables, some abbreviations are used as follows:

- GC—gestational surrogate
- IP—intended parent
- ED—egg donor (or sometimes: egg donation)
- ACA—Affordable Care Act health insurance policy
- LL—Lloyd's of London health insurance policy
- MMPI—Minnesota Multiphasic Personality Inventory test

MHB Cost Tracking Sheet for Surrogacy

Men Having Babies - Cost Tracking Sheet: USA SURROGACY
© 2015 Men Having Babies

		Not essential	Included in fees	Not provided	3rd party estimate

Stage	Function / service	CCC	Min	Max	Likely Cost
AGENCY & LEGAL			**$ 24,000**	**$ 45,000**	**$ 29,000**
Match / screen	Agency retainer		$ 12,500	$ 25,000	$ 18,000
	GC recruitment / advertising				
	GC screening and match		$ 2,200	$ 2,500	$ -
	GC Psychological screening		$ 700	$ 1,625	$ 1,000
	GC Criminal background screening		$ 100	$ 400	$ 100
	GC home visit		$ 500	$ 1,200	$ -
	GC medical records review				
	IP Psychological Evaluation			$ 500	
	IP background screening		$ 110	$ 200	$ -
	GC insurance review		$ 150	$ 1,500	$ -
	International IPs supplemental fee		$ 1,000	$ 4,900	
	Rematch fee (if needed)			$ 3,500	$ -
GC Contract	Carrier contract: legal representation for IP		$ 1,500	$ 5,000	$ 3,000
	Carrier contract: legal representation for GC				$ 1,000
Journey	Escrow / Trust services (setup + monthly or flat)		$ 750	$ 1,700	$ 1,200
	Management of bill payments / disbursement		$ 120	$ 1,500	$ -
	Case management / journey coordination			$ 3,800	$ -
	Coordination with clinic (screening / IVF)				$ -
	Travel coordination			$ 2,000	$ -
	Psychological support of IPs				$ -
	Psychological support of GC		$ 270	$ 2,500	$ 1,000
	Birth arrangements guidance / coordination			$ 950	$ -
Finalization	Legal representation for parental rights		$ 2,500	$ 5,500	$ 4,000
	GC's legal representation for parental rights		$ 600	$ 1,500	$ -
	Coordination - DNA testing, passport issuance, etc.		$ 1,500	$ 2,000	$ -
	DNA testing fees		$ 500	$ 600	$ -
	Court fees		$ 150	$ 500	$ -
GC COMPENSATION AND EXPENSES			**$ 28,000**	**$ 56,000**	**$ 40,000**
Compensation	GC compensation		$ 17,000	$ 35,000	$ 29,000
	GC extra for good insurance		$ 2,000	$ 4,000	$ -
	Life Insurance Policy (+estate planning?)		$ 175	$ 1,000	$ 600
	Disability Insurance		$ 800	$ 1,200	$ -
Screening	Screening travel - GC (fair, transfers, hotel and m		$ 1,000	$ 1,500	$ 1,250
	Screening travel - partner supplement	and GC parnered	$ 500	$ 1,000	$ 750
	Screening - lost wages and / or childcare		$ -	$ 420	$ 350
	Surrogate Mock Cycle fee				
Transfer	Transfer Fee		$ 500	$ 1,500	$ 500
	Transfer travel - GC (fair, transfers, hotel and me		$ 1,000	$ 1,500	$ 1,250
	Transfer travel - companion supplement	and GC parnered	$ 500	$ 1,000	$ 750
	Transfer lost wages or childcare		$ -	$ 420	$ 350
Pregnancy	Monthly allowance for expenses		$ 2,400	$ 3,600	$ 2,400
	Maternity Clothing Allowance		$ 500	$ 1,000	$ 800
	Misc. negotiated expenses				$ -
	Local travel (if not covered by allowance)				
	Bed Rest - lost wages or child care	and Bed rest	$ 700	$ 6,000	$ 1,400
	GC Fee for Multiple Pregnancy		$ 2,000	$ 5,000	$ 5,000
	Additional maternity clothing for Multiples		$ 250	$ 1,000	$ 250
	Additional housekeeping for Multiples			$ 5,000	$ -
	GC Fee for Invasive Procedures	GC proceadure #	$ 500	$ 1,000	$ -
	GC fee for Selective Reduction or Termination	GC proceadure #	$ 500	$ 1,500	$ -
Delivery	Post-birth bed rest / lost wages	C-Section	$ 1,400	$ 2,800	$ 1,400
	GC Fee for Cesarean Section	C-Section	$ 1,500	$ 3,000	$ -
	GC Fee for Loss of Reproductive Organs	Loss of Organs	$ 2,500	$ 5,000	$ -
NON-IVF INSURANCE & MEDICAL			**$ -**	**$ 30,000**	**$ 10,000**
	Maternity / delivery co-pays and deductibles		$ -	$ 7,000	$ 3,000
	Newborn co-pays and deductibles		$ -	$ 3,000	$ 2,000
	Complications insurance				
	GC medical Insurance - buy a standard policy		$ 3,000	$ 4,200	
	GC medical Insurance - buy a Lloyds backup pol		$ 3,000	$ 5,000	$ 5,000
	GC medical Insurance - buy Lloyds's full policy		$ 28,000	$ 30,000	
	Out of pocket delivery (when buying LL)				
	Health Insurance for newborn - ACA				
	Health Insurance for newborn - Lloyds				
	Out of pocket for Newborn - (when buying LL)				
TOTAL	(excluding twins)		**$ 52,000**	**$ 131,000**	**$ 79,000**

MHB Cost Tracking Sheet for IVF with Egg Donor

Men Having Babies - Cost Tracking Sheet: USA IVF and ED
© 2015 Men Having Babies

			Not essential	Included in fees	Not provided	3rd party estimate
		CCC		**GENERIC**		
Stage	**Function / service**		**Min**	**Max**	**Likely Cost**	

Stage	Function / service	CCC	Min	Max	Likely Cost
EGG DONOR NON-CLINIC COSTS			$ 7,000	$ 16,000	$ 11,000
Matching and legal	Agency /matching fees		$ 1,350	$ 2,500	$ 2,000
	Egg Donation International IP's Fee			$ 1,000	$ -
	Social worker evaluation		$ 125	$ 350	$ -
	Psychologist screening		$ 150	$ 500	$ 150
	Criminal background check			$ 50	
	MMPI testing			$ 50	
	Drug Testing			$ 125	
ED compensation / expenses	Egg Donor stipend		$ 4,500	$ 10,000	$ 8,000
	Complications insurance		$ 245	$ 500	$ 300
	Egg Donation Contract Legal Fee (IP rep)				
	Egg Donor's legal representation		$ 400	$ 500	$ -
	Escrow / fund management for ED			$ 150	$ -
	ED travel and other expenses (local)		$ 350	$ 500	$ -
	ED travel and other expenses (non local)		$ 1,000	$ 5,000	$ -
	ED satellite clinic monitoring (if non local)		$ 2,000	$ 5,000	$ -
MEDICAL SCREENING			$ 3,500	$ 14,000	$ 8,000
ED medical Screening	Pre-admission screening (baseline / often at local OB)				
	Dr. interview		$ 150	$ 250	
	Physical exam		$ 200	$ 250	
	FDA-required bloodwork (twice?)		$ 750	$ 4,000	$ 1,500
	Standard genetic screening		$ 200	$ 1,000	$ 1,000
	Enhanced genetic screening				
GC medical Screening	Pre-admission screening (often at local OB)				
	Group Consultation with IP's/Psychologist facilitation		$ 175	$ 1,000	
	Dr. interview/nurse consults				
	GC physical / blood and uterine testing				
	GC FDA-required bloodwork		$ 475	$ 1,975	$ 750
	Partner FDA-required bloodwork	GC parnered	$ 750	$ 1,200	$ 750
IPs medical Screening	Dr. interview				
	IP Psychological Assessment (PAI / MMPI)		$ 175	$ 500	
	Physical examination				
	Semen analysis (insurance?)		$ 100	$ 448	
	Semen cryopreservation		$ 750	$ 3,000	
	FDA-required bloodwork - one sperm source (insurance?)		$ 500	$ 1,200	$ 750
	FDA-required bloodwork - 2nd sperm source		$ 500	$ 3,000	$ 750
	Shipping of FDA kit		$ 300	$ 325	
	Genetic counseling				$ 500
	Enhanced genetic screening				$ 350
IVF TREATMENT			$ 20,000	$ 30,000	$ 24,000
IVF Program Fees			$ 13,500	$ 17,500	$ 17,000
ED treatment / monitoring	Egg donor cycle coordination fee		$ 2,000	$ 4,000	
	Medications for egg donor		$ 3,500	$ 7,000	$ 4,000
	Monitoring - office visits for egg donor		$ 200	$ 3,500	
	Monitoring - ultrasound examinations		$ 600	$ 1,400	
	Monitoring -bloodwork		$ 300	$ 550	
GC treatment / monitoring	GC cycle coordination fee			$ 1,000	
	GC sonohystogram and mock cycle		$ 250	$ 970	
	Medications for carrier		$ 850	$ 1,600	$ 1,000
	Ultrasound & blood for alignment and suppression (outside clinic)				$ 1,500
	Pregnancy tests				
	Monitoring of carrier through 12th week of pregnancy				
IVF Procedures	Egg retrieval with ultrasound guidance		$ 1,475	$ 2,530	
	Anesthesia for egg retrieval		$ 425	$ 600	$ 600
	Embryo transfer with ultrasound guidance		$ 1,200	$ 1,960	
IVF Lab fees	Oocyte identification & recovery		$ 1,100	$ 3,150	
	Oocyte culture, fertilization, blastocyst		$ 2,080	$ 4,800	
	IVF and lab fees for second biological father		$ 2,000	$ 4,800	
	ICSI			$ 2,250	
	Assisted hatching		$ 530	$ 2,300	
	Embryo cryopreservation (freezing)		$ 500	$ 2,300	
	Embryo storage - first year		$ 600	$ 1,200	
	Genetic Testing/Pre-implantation genetic diagnosis (PGD)		$ 1,200	$ 6,250	
	Gender selection			$ 5,000	
TOTAL			$ 30,500	$ 60,000	$ 43,000
FROZEN EMBRYO CYCLE			$ 4,300	$ 8,000	$ 6,500
Frozen embryo transfer	Embryo thawing				
	Embryo transfer with ultrasound guidance				
	Additional monitoring of carrier through 12th week of pregnancy				
	Medications for carrier				$ 1,000

ART Financing Options

Having a child is expensive enough and the finances associated with ART can certainly cut into some couples' own living standards as well as college savings funds for the contemplated child. While some states mandate that medical insurance provides a form of coverage for ART, most medical insurance does *not* cover the costs of ART, thus leaving patients to pay for most of the procedures and medicals out of pocket. Since ART is not just for the "rich and famous" but is instead for all walks of life, including those with financial challenges, it is comforting to be aware that there are options to help pay for these procedures, while protecting your own personal savings. In addition to the Internet, a resource to learn about financing options is through your fertility clinic. Many clinics have finance departments that guide patients to resources that may be available to assist with and assuage the expenses.

Discounted Multi-Cycle and/or Refund Programs

While it is unpleasant to accept that you may need to try multiple rounds of IVF before being successful, many practices offer "refund" and/or "discounted multi-cycle" IVF programs for patients that qualify. Fertility clinics with these programs offer plans that provide patients with multiple IVF cycles, including the use of an egg donor (a certain amount of fresh and frozen embryo transfers) for a single, discounted fee that costs about 30 to 40 percent less than the treatment plan if you were to pay for it on a cycle-by-cycle basis. Some plans provide that if you do not bring home a child, you can receive all or a portion of your money back after a certain number of attempts. When considering this type of program, inquire whether or not you can withdraw from the program at any time, if you can transfer it to other fertility clinics, and what costs are not included in the program. Typical costs not included are normal prescreening tests, medication, surgeries not related to IVF, recruitment, or purchase fees for donor sperm or donor egg.

Grants, Financial Aid, and Scholarships

There are some incredible organizations that help provide financial assistance to those wanting to build a family through ART but having financial difficulty in doing so. Some organization are focused on helping certain groups of people such as same-sex couples, religious affiliations, those suffering from cancer, or those that are financially need based. Some states have in-state assistance programs available to residents to pay for certain ART expenses.

NOTE

There are numerous grant and financial aid programs available throughout the country. Some examples of organizations that provide financial guidance and assistance to those struggling with ART that are explained in detail within this guide include Fertile Action, Men Having Babies, and the International Council on Infertility Information Dissemination.

Corporate Benefits

Some large corporations include adoption, surrogacy, and other ART costs as a benefit of employment. If you or your spouse are fortunate enough to be employed by such a company, check with your human resources contact for details on the program.

While company policies are always changing, examples of previous infertility and adoption friendly employers include, but are not limited to, Abbott, Ace Hardware, Kinkos, and Marriott, just to name a few, which offer benefits such as payment for ART medications, coverage for ART medical procedures, sometimes offering coverage for multiple attempts, and adoption assistance. For a comprehensive list of companies that may offer infertility or adoption benefits, visit the International Council on Infertility Information Dissemination's website at http://www.inciid.org/companies-that-may-offer-infertility-benefits.

Fertility Assistance Loans

While you may think of loans as an option for purchasing a home or attending college or graduate school, some financial institutions offer unsecured loans (the bank cannot foreclose on your house for nonpayment) for fertility treatments for qualifying patients. In addition to specific fertility assistance loans, homeowners may be able to take out a home equity loan to finance infertility treatment. For any type of loan, lenders will use your credit history to determine your eligibility, how much you can borrow, and the terms of the loan. When considering a fertility assistance loan, be sure to confirm what the loan covers as many loans exclude medications or certain procedures.

Legal Implications of ART

What Is a Legal Parent?

It is imperative that intended parents utilizing assisted reproductive technology (ART) ensure that they are deemed the legal parents of the resultant child. As mainly seen in situations of egg/sperm/embryo donation use and surrogacy, the parental rights of the intended parents are challenged and jeopardized when certain legal safeguards are not carefully considered and thoroughly addressed.

Why is it important to be deemed a legal parent? Family law shareholder Mark Rabinowitz with Greenspoon Marder, P.A. (http://www.gmlaw.com), discusses the responsibility of legal parents and what happens if you are not deemed a legal parent in the context of ART:

> Reproductive technology has impacted the parental rights of children born from these processes. A legal parent is generally defined as one who has a child born to him or her during an intact marriage. When a child is born to parents of an intact marriage the legal duty to support that child and to have rights of visitation or contact presumptively rests with the parties to the marriage. Additionally, being a legal parent means that the parent will have visitation rights, the ability to make medical decisions relating to the child, the child will have the automatic right to inherit from the legal parents (absent contrary directions in a will), and the ability to make lifestyle decisions for the child such as school and extracurricular activities. Without being deemed a legal parent, the ability to make important decisions regarding the child's future does not exist. Legal presumption may be challenged with parents who chose to engage in ART practices.
>
> In cases where married couples desire to have children through egg, sperm, or embryo donation or surrogacy the greatest protection they can afford themselves to protect their interest is to engage in detailed contracts in accord with state laws. Absent such contracts, the couple risk legal challenges to their status as legal parents by the surrogate or donor. Surrogates and donors

How would you like to go through this entire process, through the thick and thin of it financially and emotionally, only to find at the end that there is a question as to your parental rights to the resultant child? You wouldn't. A patient considering medical assistance in building a family should consult with an ART attorney for the legal implications that need to be considered, along with a trusts and estates attorney to properly protect the contemplated/unborn child.

CAUTION

have filed lawsuits alleging their legal status as the legal parent of the child and seeking child support or visitation rights with the child.

Absent a specific contract detailing the married couples rights with respect to their child, the right to raise and care for the child can be challenged in a dissolution of marriage proceeding. To date challenges have arisen between same-sex and heterosexual couples who have engaged surrogates and donors. The challenges have included the right to visit or have contact with children conceived by donors and surrogates during their intact marriages. In those cases, the contracts entered into by the parties and the surrogates and donors are scrutinized.

State Law Considerations with ART

We tell any potential client considering ART, including surrogacy or egg, sperm, or embryo donation that as ART is a relatively new legal concept, the law is unsettled and that much of the ART world remains shockingly unregulated. Each state and country has its own laws or sometimes no law at all relating to ART. The *New York Times* calls the phenomenon, where surrogacy is legal in one state and a criminal offense in another, a "maze of laws, state by state."[3]

An illustration of the legal confusion and resultant chaos that comes into play when states have different laws regarding ART is the situation of a surrogate entering into a surrogacy contract in one state where surrogacy is legal and then the surrogate flees to another state to deliver the baby where surrogacy contracts are not enforceable; this may jeopardize the intended parents' parental rights to the child. It is a terrifying thought.

The legal landscape in the United States is changing quickly relating to surrogacy. A handful of states, considered to be surrogacy-friendly states, have specific laws permitting surrogacy; however, each state varies greatly in the limitations relating to the practice. Many states are reluctant to pass laws governing surrogacy and the majority of states have no controlling law. Compare this to restrictive states where it is a crime to compensate a surrogate. Within these diverse approaches to determine the legal parent of a child born through surrogacy within the United States and around the world, it is evident how different outcomes can occur depending on where the child is born.

---

[3]http://www.nytimes.com/2014/09/18/us/surrogates-and-couples-face-a-maze-of-laws-state-by-state.html?_r=0

Not only is the surrogacy contract process different in each state, but the legal proceedings required keep off or remove the surrogate as the mother from the birth certificate and name the intended parents as the legal parents differs across the country. While court intervention is not necessarily required for gestational surrogacy arrangements, naming the intended parents as the legal parents may need to be established through a court action. Some states allow a prebirth order naming the intended parents as the legal parents so that the birth certificate never lists the surrogate as the birth mother. Some states require postbirth parentage proceedings to issue a new birth certificate removing the surrogate as the legal mother and naming the intended parents as the legal parents, and some states require a form of an adoption proceeding to terminate a surrogate's parental rights and name the intended parents as the legal parents.

So what law applies to ART? Generally, the law of the state where the child is born is the applicable law. However, when a surrogate, donor, and intended parent(s) are located in different states or even countries, or the IVF procedures occur in different jurisdictions, it is advisable to consider the laws of where the IVF procedures occurred and also consider the state/s where all parties are located to determine if any of the locations raise legal concerns as to confirming the parental rights once the child is born. An articulation in your surrogacy contract is a great way to assert your intention for the law of a certain jurisdiction to govern your case, but that doesn't necessarily mean that the jurisdiction you choose has jurisdiction over your specific matter. Yeah, it's confusing.

Constitutional Considerations with ART

Within the United States, ART is governed by state law. Individual states are left to chart their own course. That being said, the US Constitution places limits on the range of choices available to the states. The application of the Constitution to ART law is always evolving as new legal situations arise in the ART world.

So, you may be asking, what is an example of a way the Constitution can trump a state's surrogacy laws? The major right relates to the surrogate's right to make decisions as they relate to her body—the constitutional right to bodily autonomy. Even if your surrogacy contract provides that the surrogate will terminate the pregnancy if a doctor determines there is a genetic abnormality or other problem, the surrogate has the right under the Constitution to change her mind based on the constitutional right to her body and the only remedy the intended parents may have is to recover the money paid to the surrogate and third parties (which may be difficult to get back from the surrogate). The intended parents cannot force a surrogate to terminate the pregnancy, and the intended parents will need to accept custody of the child regardless of any impairment.

Another constitutional right seen in the ART context is the intended parents' constitutional right to procreate. This protection has come into play recently in the same-sex family-building context where, for example, a woman who donates her egg (biological mother) to her lesbian partner who subsequently delivers the child (birth mother), should not be considered merely a donor if her intent is to be the legal parent of the child. Therefore, if a state's laws do not permit a same-sex couple to act as intended parents in an egg donation situation, the biological mother's constitutional rights could be deprived as she has the constitutionally protected right to procreate and be a parent.

Surrogacy Contracts and Related Legal Documents

There are many types of contracts involved relating to ART. These should be executed prior to the start of any medical procedures that a donor and/or surrogate will undergo in preparation for the retrieval or embryo transfer. Such contracts include gestational surrogacy contracts, traditional surrogacy contracts, egg, sperm, or embryo donation contracts, embryo disposition forms, and trust and estate documents, just to name a few.

Do not copy a contract you find online or even the language in this book! Many factors need to be considered and customized when determining what type of surrogacy contract and legal processes an intended parent needs to follow when using a surrogate. The process and type of contract will depend on certain variables, such as whether or not it is a traditional *vs.* gestational surrogacy and whether or not the intended parents are single, married, or a same-sex couple (married or unmarried), among many other factors. Depending on the state where the surrogacy is occurring, the name of the contract may change, and the process in naming the intended parents, as the legal parents, differs accordingly. Regardless, the general legal principals in a surrogacy contract are similar across state lines to protect all parties involved.

When contemplating using a surrogate, it is critical to obtain experienced legal services throughout the process. An attorney needs to be retained to prepare a contract between the intended parents and the surrogate. Many states require this type of contract even before the embryo transfer takes place and most fertility clinics will not start medications until the aforementioned contract is fully executed. The purpose of the contract is to address the many questions that arise during the pregnancy and a solid contract prevents disputes from occurring between the parties by laying out all of the financial terms.

There is no "standard" or "boilerplate" form contract! Certainly there is some language that appears in every contract (as discussed below), but every case needs to be addressed with care by a competent legal professional who understands how to juxtapose the law with the process and also with the various parties and entities involved in the process. Here's an example: If your lawyer knows that the judge who has your case likes things done a certain way or that the clinic you're using requires certain types of releases or notices prior to getting down to the process, that knowledge can save you time, money, and aggravation and might even save the whole process from failing due to unnecessary delays. As you will see, in surrogacy, timing is everything.

> **NOTE**
>
> Like a snowflake, no two ART cases are the same.

Surrogacy is a very specific area of law. It is *crucial* that the intended parents retain an attorney experienced in ART law to represent them to prepare the surrogacy contract. Additionally it is advised that the intended parents offer and pay for a separate ART attorney to represent the surrogate during the contract negotiation stage. In fact, don't be surprised if your IVF clinic or attorney actually *requires* that the surrogate have her own attorney to guide her through the contract. This small additional expense is for the protection of all parties, not least of all, protects *you*.

Descriptions of some of the more notable provisions in a surrogacy contract follow below:

Purpose and Intent

The beginning of a surrogacy contract includes recitals that set out the purpose of the contract and defines each party's intent to either give up parental rights to the child (surrogate and surrogate's spouse or possibly her partner) and to accept parental rights to the child (intended parents) and introduces said parties with regard to age, marital status, and place of residence. The parties' obligations to either terminate parental rights or accept such parental rights are addressed at length within the surrogacy contract as well and the surrogate and her spouse or at times a partner will agree to sign whatever documents necessary or attend any court proceedings to make sure that the child she carries ends up being the legal child of the intended parents.

Physical Examinations and Psychological Evaluations

All parties to the contract agree to participate in medical and psychological evaluation and counseling sufficient to assure that they fully understand the risks, benefits, and appropriateness of their participation in the surrogacy arrangement. The surrogate and surrogate's spouse (and at times, a surrogate's unmarried partner) also agrees to execute medical releases and authorizations to permit the intended parents access to all medical records and information as deemed necessary or appropriate for such purposes as may be related to the surrogacy process. This means that no medical information relating to the pregnancy can be kept confidential.

Prenatal Care of Surrogate

Many potential intended parents are concerned about how the surrogate will act during the pregnancy and whether she will take good care of herself and the child. Based on the constitutional provisions set out above, while you cannot force a surrogate to conduct herself in a certain manner as it relates to her body, a contract can set out reasonable guidelines for a surrogate to follow whereby a breach of such requirements could result in a financial obligation of the surrogate. When signing a surrogacy contract, the surrogate agrees to maintain optimum health and refrain from activities which could cause injury to her or impair her ability to become pregnant or to carry a child.

Child's Name and Birth Certificate Process

A surrogacy contract must have provisions establishing what state law will apply and the applicable anticipated process for the determination of parental rights for the intended parents. Each state has very different procedures on how to handle the birth certificate process.

Termination of the Pregnancy and Selective Reduction

While the Constitution places limits on the intended parents' ability to force a surrogate to terminate or not terminate a pregnancy, a surrogacy contract will set out the parties' wishes as to how to handle the situation of a birth defect discovered during the pregnancy. This contract language provides the intended parents with a contract remedy of monetary damages against the surrogate if she does not respect the wishes of the intended parents.

The surrogate has the right to abort or terminate the pregnancy if she wants to. She has the right to *not* abort, terminate, or selectively reduce if she doesn't want to, even if the intended parents and all the doctors in the world are telling her she should or must. This is one of the many leaps of faith that are taken when engaging a surrogate to carry your pregnancy, and this underscores the importance of having an experienced surrogacy professional engaged to do the vetting and matching with the surrogate, as opposed to finding one online. While success stories do exist from families who took the DIY approach to matching, there are horror stories, too. Govern yourself accordingly.

> **TIP**
>
> When I'm reviewing a GSA with a surrogate, or any kind of contract with any client at all, I explain the following: When you enter into a contract you have two choices: a) perform or b) breach. Nobody can make you do anything you don't want to do, even if you agreed to do it. However, with a breach comes with consequences, and the consequences for breaching a surrogacy contract are NOT WORTH IT! DO NOT enter into this contract if you are not 1,000 percent sure you fully intend and have the ability to do exactly what you're promising.

Payment of Surrogate Expenses and Payment Terms

The money for a surrogate is typically held by an independent third party called an escrow agent who disburses all payments to the surrogate in accordance with the terms of the surrogacy contract. The intended parents are required to keep a certain amount of money in the escrow account at all times to ensure there is enough money available to pay the surrogate throughout and after the contract as required by the terms. A surrogate typically receives a few smaller payments prior to becoming pregnant, such as when her injectable medications start and at the embryo transfer; however, the main payment of her fee typically begins when her pregnancy is confirmed and continues to be paid to her every four weeks as the pregnancy progresses.

The payment provisions in the surrogacy contract set out the financial terms such as what payments are lawful to the surrogate, how much the surrogate will receive for her services, and when the payments are to be made. Common payments made to a surrogate include her reasonable living expenses, her "fee," an allowance for maternity clothes, payment for the start of her injectable medications and embryo transfer, payment of her attorney fees, and payment for or reimbursement of all medical, hospital, and pharmaceutical and laboratory expenses associated with the IVF, hospital, and delivery.

Confidentiality and Contact with Child

With the popularity of social media, an intended parent who wants to keep the nature of their surrogacy arrangement private may have concerns that the surrogate may post pictures disclosing identifying information of the intended parents and of the pregnancy. A surrogacy contract should have strict confidentiality language requiring all parties to agree to take all reasonable precautions to maintain the strictest confidentiality with regard to the contract. The contract should restrict the parties from providing any information regarding the identities of the parties or the contemplated child, the results of any medical testing relating to any of the parties or the child, or terms of the contract, to the public, news media, on social media, or other individuals or entities without the express prior written permission and consent in each instance of all the parties.

Legal Complications Relating to Surrogacy

Surrogate Refuses to Terminate or Reduce the Pregnancy If There Is a Problem

A significant legal risk when considering using a surrogate is that the surrogate has the sole source of consent with respect to her body under the US Constitution. In the event during the pregnancy the doctor determines that there is a birth defect or genetic abnormality and the parties' contract provides that the surrogate agrees to terminate the pregnancy, the surrogate can change her mind and decide not to terminate the pregnancy. The intended parents have to accept custody of the child, regardless of any type of impairment, and the only remedy against the surrogate is to stop payment to the surrogate and attempt to recover the money they paid to her and third parties; this may be difficult to collect. This concept is also applicable in context of any invasive testing. The surrogate may refuse the test even after previously agreeing to it (i.e., amniocentesis). Also important is if three or more embryos implant in the uterus of the surrogate and the intended parents want to selectively reduce the number of embryos. While the parties may agree, both verbally and in the contract to selectively reduce the pregnancy, no conversation or contract is binding; the surrogate has the final say and can change her mind on selective reduction.

Surrogate Changes Her Mind to Give up the Child

This problem is more commonly seen with traditional surrogacy whereby the surrogate has a genetic connection to the child. In some states, when a surrogate uses her own egg, she has a window of time after the birth to change her mind in giving up the child to the intended parents, similar to an adoption. Also, with surrogacy, having a crazy quilt of laws throughout the United States, there is risk that the surrogate may flee a surrogacy friendly state during the pregnancy and move to a state where it is illegal. While the parties' surrogacy contract designates the state law that is to apply to the surrogacy process, this may still cause added legal expense to the intended parents who then need to enforce the contract and may have added legal proceedings to name them as the legal parents upon birth of the child.

Intended Parents Change Their Minds to Take the Child

There is always the risk that the intended parents will not accept custody of the child. There have been reported cases, for example, where the intended parents refused to accept custody of the child born via a surrogate when the child was born with a problem, such as Down syndrome.

Surrogate's Breach of the Contract

There is always the risk that the surrogate will not follow the terms of the contract such as taking her required medications, eating healthy or living a healthy lifestyle, etc. Regardless of the impairment to the child caused by the surrogate's poor choices during pregnancy, the intended parents have to accept the child, no matter what.

As shown above, there are legal risks to consider with the surrogacy process. ART attorney, and former intended mother, Jessica Geller, Esq. (http://www.glam-law.com) shares that while most surrogacy journeys are positive, in her years of experience with ART law, there is always the chance that sticky situations can happen:

> I have assisted dozens of families since 2008 with surrogacy and pre-planned adoptions. Many are lucky enough like me to find a friend or family member to assist, which is the best possible outcome, as long as there are clear boundaries discussed at the beginning through a trained psychologist. It is natural for the surrogate who is a friend or family member, and who will likely be involved or at least informed about the child after birth to have more of an attachment to the child than a surrogate who was unknown prior to the surrogacy. However, it is important that intended parents communicate as much as possible before, during, and after the process to ensure the surrogate does not and will not have unrealistic or intrusive expectations about her role.
>
> Most of my experiences have been very positive. Most surrogacy experiences are successful and the intended parents have good relationships with their surrogate and her family. However, I have had a few experiences that did not go so smoothly. There was one surrogate that was found by police six months pregnant on the side of the road, intoxicated. Thankfully, the child was born safely with no apparent abnormalities. The contract with the surrogate should always have a clause that if the surrogate breaches the contract, she will not receive the balance of payments due. Intended parents should have someone in the area, if they are not local, to monitor the surrogate if it becomes necessary. Criminal background

searches, psychological evaluations, and medical exams should prevent a surrogate with substance abuse issues from being selected.

Another surrogate backed out of the process after getting paid a significant deposit against my advice because an attorney later advised her that since she was only here on a green card, she was at risk of deportation, which would complicate the surrogacy (deportation would indeed complicate matters as the laws of other states and countries regarding surrogacy differ and may not be as advantageous as Florida law; however this surrogate was married to a US citizen with three children and had been here for thirteen years, so her attorney's assertions were disingenuous). The lesson is to carefully screen your surrogate through experienced surrogacy agencies and listen to and follow your attorney's advice to ensure the best outcome possible.

Legal Issues Relating to Donated Egg, Sperm, or Embryos

As the technology for the freezing of eggs, sperm, and embryos improves allowing for the donation of such genetic material, the legal challenges equally increase presenting new and unique dilemmas for donors and recipients. Do you want to be the guy who donated sperm only to be slapped with a paternity lawsuit from the biological mother of the child who's carrying around your DNA? I didn't think so. That's why it's so important to discuss these matters with an experienced ART attorney before diving too deep into the ART world.

Legislatures and courts have only begun to look at the ramifications of egg, sperm, and embryo donation, with only a handful of states having passed legislation pertaining to such donations. The two main legal concerns that this book addresses relating to genetic donation is (1) what legal ramifications come into play when using donated genetic material to make sure the donor is not deemed a legal parent, and (2) what happens to the donated genetic material after it is frozen and the couple that creates the frozen material later separates, gets divorced, or dies.

Donated Egg, Sperm, or Embryos and Challenges of Parental Rights

It is generally the legal understanding that a donor is not a parent of a child conceived by means of ART. If a person is deemed a donor, they will not have any rights or duties (including child support) to the child conceived by use of the donated material unless the parties' contract provides otherwise. A donor of genetic material is from someone known to the intended parents and they have a relationship to the donor, such as a friend or family member, or the intended parents have no relationship to or knowledge of the donor, referred to as an "anonymous donor." While legal challenges can arise with both known and anonymous donors, most of the reported cases of disputes documented in the United States occur with known donors. Remember that each state has different laws relating to donors and it is important to consult with an ART attorney in the state where the procedure occurs, where the parties are located, and where the birth will occur, before conducting any form of fertility procedure. This is of paramount importance when working with a known donor.

The Known Donor

In some court cases around the county, especially in earlier ART cases, the fact that a donor is known to the intended parents has an impact on whether or not the donor has parental rights to the resulting child. For example, a famous ART case from 1986 under an old California law determined that because a man, who provided his sperm directly to a woman and her partner was *known* to the women, and because they were not aware of the legal steps necessary of delivering the sperm to a physician (which was required by the law at that time to consider someone a donor), the man, who provided his sperm, was deemed the legal father of the resulting child, even though the intent of the parties was for the man to be a donor and not a legal father. Without a contract between the parties to demonstrate how they wanted to treat the donated sperm, and because they did not follow the state's legal requirements to make someone a donor, this man was deemed to be the legal father.

Another example of the importance of knowing your state law before giving or receiving donated genetic material is to know the rules as to the method of conception and whether this impacts the parties' parental rights and obligations to the future child. A fact pattern straight out of the movie *The Big Chill* took place in a Florida case, wherein a woman wanted to get pregnant in the "usual and customary manner" (civilized legal jargon for "having sex") and did not want to use artificial insemination. She asked her friend, a known donor, to be the biological father by having sex with her. In the parties' contract, it provided that if the woman became pregnant, she would have sole custody of the child, responsible for all expenses and would refrain from placing the man's name on the birth certificate. The contract essentially expressed the parties' intent that the man was merely a sperm donor and not intended to be the legal father. Fast forward ten years after the birth of the child, and the woman sued the man who provided his sperm for paternity seeking child support. The man's position essentially was, "No way. Look at the contract. . . . We agreed that I was only providing the sperm and was not to have any parental rights the child . . . and isn't ten years a long time to be asking for support?" The Florida court held that a person is only considered a donor (with no parental rights) if they donate their genetic material with the use of reproductive technology. If a party wants to help someone else have a child with no child support obligations, they cannot do so by having sex and waiving parental rights in a contract. They must utilize some form of documented reproductive technology assistance in order for the donor laws to apply. Therefore, despite the parties' efforts to waive the man's parental rights by setting the intention in a contract, since the court focused on the method of conception by way of sex as opposed to IVF or an IUI, the man who thought he was just donating his sperm ended up being the legal father to a ten-year-old child.

There are more cases similar to the ones above in the United States where challenges to parental rights are filed after a child is born to determine whether someone is considered a donor and legal stranger to a child or should be deemed a parent with all the rights and support obligations. Even if the court doesn't distinguish between whether a donor is known or unknown, an important consideration a court looks at is the *intent* of the parties when a donor donated their egg or sperm to intended parents. If the intent is properly documented in a written contract and stated that the donor had no intention of being a legal parent, and it is clear they were donating something without any expectation to be a parent, then that assists the court in deciding that the donor should not have any parental rights to the child. It is much more apparent as it relates to known donors versus when someone obtains an anonymously donated egg or sperm. The intent of the donor and the recipient is to exclude the donor from paternity; however, the problem comes into play (for known or anonymous donors) when the parties do not properly document this intention in a contract. Without a clear expression of the parties' intent, it can lead to a "he said, she said" dispute; thus leaving the court to make a factual determination to figure out what was the intent of the parties.

Contracts for Donated Egg, Sperm, or Embryos

Some states do not enforce donor contracts while many states actually require a legal contract directly between recipients and donors. Even if you live in a state where donor contracts are not enforceable under state law, it is always the best practice to have a written and signed contract setting out the parties' intent when genetic material is donated. A written contract will assist a court in understanding the intent of the parties. It is much better to have something in writing signed by the parties than to rely on verbal promises or a handshake.

Many fertility clinics provide their own donor contracts. When using donated genetic material without a clinic's contract, typically seen with egg donor agencies or through known donors, it is recommended for the intended parents to offer the donor of genetic material to have an ART attorney that is separate from the ART attorney representing the intended parents at the expense of the intended parents, to ensure that the donor fully understands the contract. This avoids any issues down the road with the donor claiming they did not understand what they were signing and thus protects all parties involved. Fees for the drafting attorney, representing the intended parents, and reviewing attorney representing the donor vary across the country.

Such donor contracts cover important issues such as terminating the donor's parental rights, stating that the intended parents shall assume legal responsibility for the child, defining compensation and insurance benefits for the donor, explaining damages and choice of law provisions, and addressing highly personal choices regarding future contact with the donor, medical information of the donor, and potential future meetings with offspring.

Disputes over Frozen Genetic Material When the Contributors Separate, Divorce, or Die

Genetic material such as eggs, sperm, and embryos can be frozen and used for procreation for many years. While we hope nothing happens in a relationship, over time, life happens and people break up, get divorced, and pass away. When

It's not fun stuff to think about, especially when the whole point of ART is to create a life, not think about one ending, but legally speaking, it is imperative that people freezing genetic material establish what they want to happen to frozen egg, sperm, or embryos during events such as death or divorce.

CAUTION

freezing genetic material, you will be faced with filling out daunting forms at your fertility clinic or long-term storage facility for frozen genetic material that has you check many boxes on how you want your frozen egg, sperm, or embryos treated in the event you die, your partner dies, you get divorced, and the contemplation of numerous other unforeseen circumstance. Do you want your embryos destroyed or used for research if you die? Can the other partner use a frozen embryo for procreation if you get divorced?

Where there is little law on resolving disputes over frozen embryos, if a woman freezes her eggs or man freezes his sperm, the courts in the United States have generally held that stored genetic material is subject to the ownership, control, and disposition of the person who contributed it. The reported litigation relates to what happens when a couple freezes an embryo, each with a half ownership in the embryo, and the couple then breaks up or gets divorced. The court cases address whether, upon separation or divorce of a couple who freeze embryos, one of the couples have superior rights to the embryo over the other party. Should a divorced woman in her mid-40s have a superior right to the embryos because of her age and possible difficulty she may have to create more embryos? Should the ex-husband of this woman be able to stop her from using the embryos because if she has a child, he may be responsible for child support for a child he is not prepared to father with his ex-wife?

What happens if the frozen embryos, subject to dispute, are not the genetic material of both of the intended parents but, for example, were created by a same-sex couple with one woman's egg and a man's donated sperm. Only one woman in that relationship has a genetic connection to the frozen embryo while both of them jointly intended to create the embryos together. This is the gray area that intrigues ART lawyers. For any readers going through a divorce that have frozen genetic material, it is important that you inform your attorney that you have frozen genetic material and to provide any disposition forms you may have completed at your fertility clinic or long-term storage facility so the attorney can avoid further dispute as to this frozen property and avoid any unwanted children.

Legal Issues Relating to Embryo Donation or Embryo Adoption

People going through IVF often are left with "extra" frozen embryos after their procedures that may never be used. Pursuant to a *New York Times* article, "In storage facilities across the nation, hundreds of thousands of frozen embryos—perhaps a million—are preserved in silver tanks of liquid nitrogen. Some are in storage for cancer patients trying to preserve their chance to have a family after chemotherapy destroys their fertility. But most are leftovers from the booming assisted reproduction industry."[4] These embryos can be destroyed or used for scientific research, but what are the legal considerations when, with the consent of the genetic creators of the embryo, an embryo is donated to another person or couple for procreation. When a couple uses a donated embryo, neither of the intended parents will have a genetic connection to the child, essentially mirroring a traditional adoption, however, with more control of the intended mother over the course of the pregnancy.

An embryo donor is defined as an individual or individuals, with dispositional control of an embryo, who provides it to another for gestation and relinquishes all of their present and future parental rights, inheritance rights, and responsibilities and financial obligations to the resulting child.

The process of donating embryos is regulated by the US Food and Drug Administration (FDA) to ensure that all donated embryos are free from infectious diseases and require stringent testing before the embryos can be donated. Fertility clinics also have their own standards and criteria such as age of the embryos and/ or the contributors.

Embryo donation is similar to egg or sperm donation where it can be done in an open manner where the parties know the source of the donor or it can be an anonymous donation. Legally speaking, as with egg or sperm donation, parties to an embryo donation arrangement should have the legal documentation in place to ensure that the donor is relinquishing any future rights to the resulting children and the recipient of the donated embryo assume parental rights to the resulting children.

Wills, Trust, and Estate Documents

When having a child, either through ART or the "old-fashioned way," it is important to have an estate plan in place for the contemplated children according to trusts and estates attorney David Kron, shareholder at Greenspoon Marder, P.A.:

The first question that I am asked by a prospective client is whether they "even need to have an estate plan." This comes from a frequent misconception that estate planning is only for the rich or that it is only for the elderly. In fact, estate planning comes in all shapes and sizes, all levels of complexity and is done for all types of reasons.

Having no estate plan in place could create unintended estate beneficiaries, guardianship conflicts (for families with children or for the elderly), and additional delays, fees, and court costs.

The *reasons for the need for an estate plan* may also include:

1. A child reaching the age of majority, as parents will no longer be able to perform financial transactions or make

---

[4]http://www.nytimes.com/2015/06/18/us/embryos-egg-donors-difficult-issues.html

health-related decisions, on behalf of their newly adult child. This may necessitate the need for a power of attorney, a healthcare surrogate, and a living will;

2. Distribution from a bank account. Who will receive this bank account upon the death of its owner? This may necessitate the need for a simple last will and testament, or a revocable living trust;

3. Having a new child, through surrogacy or adoption. This may necessitate not only the documents above but also brings in guardianship considerations for the minor child;

4. Other life changes, such as marriage, divorce, inheritance, the sale of a business, wealth preservation, and tax planning.

In a nutshell, any change in an individual's life could necessitate estate planning considerations.

The *types of estate planning* that may be appropriate for an individual may include a simple last will and testament, or it may include complex irrevocable and revocable living trusts and family limited partnerships. The type of planning required depends on the needs of the client, which is why it is so important for an attorney to spend some time getting to know his or her client. Determining the needs of each client is an imperative step in arriving at what components are most important to include in such client's planning. Good estate planning does not come from a "one size fits all" approach. It is a process by which a client shares his or her thoughts, concerns, and life changes. The correct provisions, language, and documents are arrived at as a result of those factors, through careful consideration and planning.

Without an estate plan in place, the death of an individual will cause his or her estate to be "intestate." An *intestate estate* is one in which there is no intended estate plan. What this means is that the state law on inheritance will control. This oftentimes causes unintended heirs to receive assets. In addition, such heirs will inherit in a manner determined by law and not by the individual. In intestacy, the assets will either be distributed outright or held for the benefit of the heirs, not based on their own situation and capabilities but according to ages set forth by the state. Furthermore, if a minor is the statutory heir, a guardian for the heir's inherited property will have to be appointed for the duration of the heir's minority. The appointment of such guardian could become an expensive process.

In addition, if an individual should become incapacitated (through illness, accident, or old age) but is still living, and there aren't any estate planning documents in place (such as a durable power of attorney, healthcare surrogate, or living will), a guardian will have to be

For all of the reasons above, I always respond to my prospective clients, when they ask that first question, that they *DO* need an estate plan. Once we move on from that first question, we begin the journey to determine what constitutes the estate plan that is right for them.

appointed for such an incapacitated individual so that decisions may be made. This could take time, cost money, and may lead to a conflict among loved ones, all of whom believe that they should be appointed as guardian. Perhaps the biggest issue for a young family, however, is the guardianship of minor children. Without a clear direction, set forth in a validly executed estate plan, many well-intentioned relatives may wind up fighting in court, as to whom will be appointed to serve as the guardian of the minor children, if a guardian is ever needed.

Posthumous Reproduction

Professor of Law at Pepperdine University School of Law, Kristine S. Knaplund, states that "the rapidly expanding use of assistive reproductive technology (ART) poses new challenges in determining who is your child, grandchild, nephew, niece, etc. Issues of inheritance when a decedent leaves no will, the meaning of 'child' in a will or trust, and many other questions, are all impacted by these societal changes."

While it once seemed like science fiction, it is possible for a person to conceive a child (without intercourse) with someone after they are deceased. This is the concept of posthumous reproduction. For example, if a married couple freezes embryos, the wife is able to use the frozen embryos with the genetics of her late husband if he dies after the embryos are created and go on to have his child. The legal issue that comes into play is whether this child conceived after the death of his biological father should be able to inherit from the late father's estate and be treated as an heir of the late father. Whether or not the child is treated as an heir could also impact the child's entitlement to Social Security benefits.

Are you catching on to the theme throughout this book? It depends on the specific state law as to how the posthumously conceived child is treated as it relates to inheriting from a deceased genetic parents' estate. Some nations have actually illegalized posthumous conception. States that have laws on this concept require that in order for the child to inherit from the decedent's estate, the decedent gamete provider (in this scenario, the late father), prior to his death, must have consented in writing to posthumous conception, or such consent must be clearly established by other evidence. Without such writing or evidence, the child may not inherit from the late father's estate. Some states do not have any laws relating to posthumous conception therefore the issue, involving the status of children who are conceived post death by use of ART, is legally ambiguous.

For anyone contemplating having a child through ART and considering freezing extra eggs, sperm or embryos, it is important to discuss the legal implications with a trusts and estates attorney to ensure that any child born through ART (while all parties or alive, or that may be born years after one of the genetic parents is deceased) is protected and can inherit from the genetic contributors' estates, if that is the intent of the parties. Examples of topics to consider when talking to a trusts and estates attorney as to posthumous conception include (i) whether the deceased parent's consent is required; (ii) what effect, if any, marriage or remarriage should have; and (iii) what time limitations should apply to be able to use the frozen genetic material.

Surrogate's Living Will

Within the surrogacy contract, a surrogate may agree to remain on life support (at the expense of the intended parents) in the event something horrible happens to the surrogate requiring life-sustaining assistance and if the doctor determines that child can be safely delivered. Some ART lawyers request that the surrogate and her spouse or partner execute a living will and medical power of attorney before the embryo transfer where the surrogate agrees to remain on life support until the child she is carrying can be safely delivered.

Employment Considerations for Intended Parents and Surrogates

When a surrogate leaves her job to deliver the baby or misses work to attend numerous doctor appointments, should she get maternity leave benefits from her employer even though she is not the legal parent of the child? Should the intended parents receive maternity leave benefits from their employer when the child is born even though the intended mother did not physically deliver the child?

According to Lisa McGlynn, Esq. (http://www.fisherphillips.com), attorney at Fisher & Phillips LLP, "There are many employment laws which deal with pregnancy-related issues . . . however, it is not always clear how these laws apply to the increasing number of individuals who are turning toward less conventional means to expand their families, such as surrogacy and infertility treatments."

McGlynn highlights some of the employment considerations when a working person is undergoing ART and their rights under certain federal employment regulations:

Under the Americans with Disabilities Act (ADA), reasonable accommodations must be provided to qualified individuals with a disability unless doing so would create an undue hardship for the employer. A disability is defined in part as a "physical or mental impairment that substantially limits one or more major life activities." Infertility, a condition which substantially limits an individual's ability to procreate, is a disability under the ADA, which would entitle employees to reasonable accommodations from their employers. Such accommodations may include leave so that the employee could undergo time-consuming fertility treatments such as in vitro fertilization (IVF).

The Equal Employment Opportunity Commission (EEOC), the agency tasked with enforcing federal laws that make it illegal to discriminate against job applicants and employees, has become involved when employers are accused of discriminating against employees undergoing fertility treatments or failing to provide reasonable accommodations for employees' infertility. For example, in 2013, the EEOC announced that it obtained a $60,000 settlement from an employer accused of discriminating against an employee due to her infertility. In that case, a manager allegedly made offensive comments to an employee after she revealed that she was undergoing infertility treatments. The employee was later terminated. This recent case shows that employees who believe they have been discriminated against due to their infertility are now actively bringing claims under the ADA and other laws against their employers.

An important consideration for employers is that under the ADA they may submit medical inquiry letters to medical providers in order to confirm the existence of a disability or to determine what reasonable accommodations may be needed. All such letters should include a notice that genetic information is not being requested. Pursuant to the Genetic Information Nondiscrimination Act (GINA), employers may not discriminate against an individual on the basis of genetic information. This may be especially important in cases involving fertility treatments, as medical disclosures could include information such as genetic screening results. By specifically stating in a medical inquiry letter that genetic information is not being requested, if any information is disclosed it would likely be considered an inadvertent disclosure under GINA.

The FMLA provides eligible employees with twelve weeks of job-protected, unpaid leave during any twelve-month period for, among other things, "the birth of a son or daughter of the employee and in order to care for such son or daughter" and "[b]ecause of the placement of a son or daughter with the employee for adoption or foster care." However, the FMLA only applies to individuals who have been employed by the same employer for at least twelve months within the preceding seven years, and have worked at least 1,250 hours during the twelve-month period immediately preceding the commencement of the leave, and where the employer has fifty or more employees within a seventy-five-mile radius.

A surrogate who delivers the child would certainly be eligible for FMLA for medical complications or incapacity resulting from her pregnancy. She would also be entitled to FMLA leave for the time needed to physically recover from childbirth. However, she generally would not be entitled to "bonding" time following childbirth as she would not be caring for the child after birth.

The intended parents would be entitled to the full twelve weeks of "bonding" time FMLA leave following the birth of the child. However, the intended parents would usually not be entitled to FMLA leave to care for the surrogate during the pregnancy.

Employees who are not eligible for FMLA will be subject to their company's policy (if there is one) regarding maternity/paternity leave. Some states, such as California, also have laws providing FMLA-like leave, which may be applicable.

Currently, there is little legal guidance as to how leave-related disputes involving surrogacy would be resolved.

The Fair Labor Standards Act (FLSA) provides that, for up to one year after a child's birth, a nursing mother must be provided a "reasonable break time" to express milk "each time such employee has need to express the milk." These breaks may be unpaid. Employers must also provide a place, other than a bathroom, for expressing milk that is shielded from view and free from intrusion.

This provision could reasonably apply to a woman who physically gave birth (regardless if the baby was placed for adoption or a part of a surrogacy arrangement) as well as to a woman who received a baby through adoption or surrogacy. (Women who have not physically given birth are sometimes still able to produce milk.) Accordingly, employers should provide break time for "nursing mothers" to express milk regardless of how they became mothers.

Escrow Accounts

When intended parents are required to make payments to either a donor or a surrogate, typically the parties do not exchange money directly. Some egg/surrogacy agencies can act as the third party to hold the money paid to the donor or surrogate, however, many times an independent third party, called an escrow company, holds the money in a federally insured bank account that is disbursed in accordance with the donor or surrogacy contract. Before making a disbursement from escrow, the escrow company will review any receipt or documents that are being requested for payment and seek the approval from the intended parents.

Tax Implications

Because tax law is extremely nuanced, when making payments to a surrogate or donor, an ART lawyer will typically suggest that the intended parents and the surrogate discuss the tax implications such payments will have for the tax payer.

While there are no reported cases on payments to surrogates being subject to income tax, the US Tax Court reached a decision that found that payments to an egg donor should be included in the donor's gross income and are not excluded from taxes owed. This was the first US case addressing the tax treatment of compensation received for the sale or donation of human eggs. In this case, an egg donor in California who received compensation for her donated eggs did not report the income from the donation when filing her taxes. However, because the egg donor agency reported the amounts to the IRS, the IRS expected the egg donor to pay taxes on the compensation. The donor argued that the money she received should be tax free and treated similar to pain and suffering payments one would receive in a personal injury settlement since she considered the money for her time, efforts, inconvenience, and pain and suffering. However, the IRS ultimately ruled that the compensation for her eggs was not exempt from her ordinary gross income and was subject to taxes. (Interestingly, the ruling included a comparison to the pain and suffering, which a professional athlete goes through in his/her career, and suggested that allowing this type of compensation to go untaxed would give every professional athlete and performer a device through which they could claim that their professional salary was compensation for pain and suffering and therefore was untaxable.)

What to Look for in an ART Attorney

ART law is always evolving and is very specialized. The last thing you want to do is have your real estate attorney friend attempt to prepare the necessary documents for the contemplated procedures as it could jeopardize your legal rights following the birth of the child. Be sure that the attorney you hire has the qualifications, expertise, and knowledge of ART before retaining them. Hiring an attorney may be a new concept for many people and while you of course want to make sure they have the legal knowledge necessary to guide you through the process, you also want to make sure you like the attorney and feel reasonably comfortable with them on a personal and professional level. Some questions to help guide those looking for an ART attorney can include:

1. Where is the ART attorney licensed to practice? Attorneys are licensed on a state-by-state basis, and if a surrogate is expecting to deliver outside the state of the lawyer's jurisdiction, that lawyer may not be able to assist you.
2. How much do they charge for legal services? Is there a retainer fee required? Are there any additional costs involved such as court filing fees, copies, or other administrative fees?
3. Does the lawyer charge a flat fee or bill hourly?
4. Does the ART lawyer's firm offer other legal services such as tax law, trusts, and estates services or immigration as all fields may be required when starting a family or considering international ART procedures?
5. What percentage of the lawyer's practice is ART law?
6. Will I be working with a lawyer or with a staff member? What is the accessibility of the lawyer?

Same-Sex Couples' Access to ART Treatment

With the advent of ART, a single person or same-sex couples can build a family and have a genetic connection to the child. Unique medical questions that need to be addressed by gay and lesbian people considering ART, such as whose sperm and egg will be used and who will carry the child. In addition to the medical logistics and psychological considerations, you always need to consider your state law to ensure that any parties who want to be legal parents will be legally protected and that any donors or surrogates are not afforded parental rights. Some states have simplified legal proceedings to place both members of a same-sex couple on the birth certificate, while other states may require a second parent adoption proceeding to name the nonbiological parent as the legal parent once the child is born. Depending on which way winds are blowing politically at any given time in your jurisdiction or and/or our country, procedures for administrative minutiae, including which box you would check on your state's birth certificate amendment form, may change from time to time.

Believe it or not, fertility clinics differ in their willingness to treat single persons, unmarried couples (both heterosexual and same-sex), and lesbian and gay couples. Clinic's restrictions on refusing to provide medical treatment to specific classes of people raises numerous ethical and moral considerations such as the fundamental right to procreate, the welfare of the resulting offspring, discrimination against unmarried people, or same-sex couples—all weighted against a clinic's right to make business decisions on who they want to treat. In addition to clinic discriminating based on marital status or sexual orientation, legally speaking, fertility clinics equally should not withhold medical care for HIV-infected patients who are willing to use recommended risk-reducing therapies.

The risk to children born to gay and lesbian people, coupled with an archaic definition of "the institution of marriage," were major fears that led to the resistance of the legal recognition of nontraditional families. Based on studies conducted by the American Psychological Association, "overall results of research suggest that the development, adjustment, and well-being of children with lesbian and gay parents do not differ markedly from that of children with heterosexual parents and that lesbian and gay parents are as likely as heterosexual parents to provide support and healthy environments for their children" (http://www.apa .org/about/policy/parenting.aspx). Based on this research, the guideline recommended by the ASRM is that of providing ART medical services equally without regard to marital, partner status, or sexual orientation. Other professional organizations agree with the nondiscriminatory access to ART including the American College of Obstetricians and Gynecologists, which said of physicians who refuse infertility services to same-sex couples.

For gay and lesbian people venturing into the ART world, be mindful of working with doctors, lawyers, agencies, and other professionals that are sensitive to the needs of same-sex couples and individuals. To guide gay and lesbian people through the maze of doctors and agencies involved with third-party assisted reproduction, the organization, Men Having Babies (http://www.menhavingbabies. org/surrogacy-directory/), through its Surrogacy Advisor Directory, provides a comprehensive directory of surrogacy service providers, surrogacy agency reviews and ratings, and fertility clinic reviews and ratings, along with feedback surveys for surrogacy parents and prospective parents.

The Surrogacy Process

Traditional Surrogacy

The word "traditional" may give you the warm and fuzzies, alluding to a sense of security and time-honored tradition. However, it is quite the opposite in the surrogacy world, as shown earlier. The inception of surrogacy began in the context of intrauterine insemination (IUI), where the surrogate would use her own egg and the sperm of the intended father (not the surrogate's partner or spouse) was injected into the surrogate's uterus. This type of surrogacy arrangement, wherein the surrogate has a genetic connection to the resulting child, is known as "traditional surrogacy." Legally, however, it's actually closer to "adoption."

Seinfeld fans may remember Jerry's mechanic pulling what he called a "Mary Beth Whitehead," in the "Bottle Deposit" episode, when Jerry's mechanic steals Jerry's car after he feels that Jerry is not caring for the car properly. Mary Beth Whitehead, a traditional surrogate in New Jersey in the early 1980s, entered into a surrogacy contract with William Stern and his wife, Elizabeth. Compensation of $10,000 was paid to Mary Beth and William's sperm was inseminated into Mary Beth, with the use of Mary Beth's egg, hence the reference of a traditional surrogate. The surrogacy contract provided that Mary Beth bring the pregnancy to term and relinquish her parental rights in favor of the Sterns. Within twenty-four hours after giving birth and transferring custody of the baby to William and Elizabeth as required by the contract, Mary Beth pulls a "Mary Beth Whitehead." Mary Beth had a change of heart, chose to forsake the $10,000, and convinced the Sterns to give the baby back to her temporarily. Mary Beth fled New Jersey and went to Florida with the baby refusing to return the baby to the Sterns. *Baby* M, the pseudonym used in the media spectacle case of *In the Matter of Baby M., 109 N.J. 396 (1988)*, raised the novel legal and social question about the meaning of parenthood and the ability to contract around issues of pregnancy and childbirth. The Sterns sued Mary Beth, and, following lengthy litigation, the court ultimately gave custody of the child to the Sterns with visitation rights granted to Mary Beth. The important legal implication regarding surrogacy is that the New Jersey Supreme Court, which viewed this arrangement as "baby-selling," invalidated the surrogacy contract as against public policy and called the intended compensation to Mary Beth "illegal, perhaps criminal, and potentially degrading to women."

With the advent of IVF, allowing for the transfer of an embryo and the ability to avoid using the surrogate's egg, the use of "traditional" surrogacy is viewed unfavorably due to the surrogate's genetic connection to the child and resultant legal problems that can arise. The intended father, who provides the sperm, should be deemed the legal father upon birth, yet because of a traditional surrogate's genetic link, the process to name the intended mother as the legal parent typically involves an adoption proceeding. In many states, after the birth of the child, the so-called "surrogate" may have a period of time to change her mind about turning over parental rights to the intended parents. Indeed, the surrogate here is more like an adoption "birth mother" insofar as her legal rights are concerned, and insofar as the proceedings necessary to finalize the process are concerned. Bottom line: We do not recommend so-called "traditional surrogacy."

Gestational Surrogacy

Fast forward to the early 1990s, and you can see the progression of the US courts and the more favorable view toward surrogacy arrangements with the use of a "gestational surrogate" or "IVF surrogacy." Unlike a traditional surrogate where the surrogate has a genetic connection to the child, a gestational surrogate has no genetic link and the source of the embryo is created by various combinations of genetic components from the intended parents and/or an egg donor and/or a sperm donor.

The process of naming the intended parents (be it a heterosexual or same-sex couple or an individual person) as the legal parents when using a gestational surrogate differs around the country and it is important to consult with an attorney in the specific state involved. Some surrogates are *required* to relinquish parental rights to the child, thus avoiding postbirth adoption proceedings; some states allow for prebirth orders naming the intended parents as the legal parents prior to birth; and some states require postbirth parentage action to be filed with the court. However, whatever the specific state's procedure may be to remove the surrogate as the legal parent and name the intended parent(s) as the legal parent, it is *dramatically* less risky when using a gestational surrogate than a traditional surrogate as it avoids a genetic association of the surrogate to the child. That being said, there is always the risk, however remote, of complications with the safer gestational surrogacy approach such as the surrogate claiming maternity based on being the birth mother and other inherit risks with surrogacy.

Why Use a Surrogate

In reading the most current issue of *US Weekly*, you may see reports of A-list celebrities using a surrogate to build their family. It may appear that they are doing so just to save their figures or be able to drink wine while "expecting"; however, nonbinding guidelines established by the American Society for Reproductive Medicine (ASRM) provide that certain medical indications ought to be present before an intended parent can use a surrogate. Examples of medical reasons to use a surrogate include a true medical condition that prevents the intended parents from carrying a child to term (for example, absence of a uterus, pulmonary hypertension), the pregnancy would present a risk to the health of the mother or child, or if a couple cannot get pregnant.

In fact, before you spend time, money, and emotional energy on the surrogacy process, consider your state's laws to determine if surrogacy must be deemed medically necessary as documented by a physician. For many suffering from infertility, using a surrogate is the last stop at the ART station. However, surrogacy may be the first stop for same-sex couples or individuals who need a third party to assist in the pregnancy process.

Reproductive endocrinologist Dr. Mark Denker with Palm Beach Fertility (http://www.palmbeachfertility.com) has the following opinion on why someone would use a surrogate and the increasing popularity of the process:

Gestational surrogacy, a derivative of traditional surrogacy incorporating IVF techniques, has been practiced in Reproductive Endocrinology for twenty-five years. It first appeared on the landscape as an option for women with who wanted to have a child inheriting their genetic information, but were unable to carry a developing baby due to contraindications to pregnancy such as obesity, cardiac disease, including pulmonary hypertension, or kidney disease. Gestational surrogacy is a good option for females who have thin endometrial linings, recurrent uterine fibroids, congenital uterine abnormalities, absent uterus, or who have undergone multiple failed IVF cycles. The increasing use and popularity of gestational surrogacy is testament to its success from both the technological and societal perspectives. Recently, successful advent of in vitro fertilization embryo transfer procedures and further refinement of embryo freezing techniques such as blastocyst vitrification (embryo freezing) have propelled gestational surrogacy into the mainstream. Gestational surrogacy has expanded the treatment options for couples, single, and same-sex couples, and women with medical indications. It is safe, effective, and should be part of every fertility specialist's treatment offerings.

The Baby Steps of Surrogacy

Consult with an ART Attorney

As you can see from reading this book, each state has different laws regarding surrogacy and the issues surrounding the concept and process. Some states make it an actual crime to compensate a surrogate, while others have surrogacy friendly laws that provide guidelines on compensation to surrogates and set clear rules on how those using a surrogate, commonly referred to as the commissioning couple or intended parents, can be named as the legal parents of the child without having to go through an adoption or other means of finalizing parental rights.

Selecting the Surrogate

Intended parents may locate a surrogate on their own (i.e., Internet, friends, family) or through fertility clinics or surrogacy agencies. An agent acts as your advocate and has the ability to (i) provide you quickly with numerous prescreened surrogate candidates; (ii) address many details you do not realize are important, such as asking the right questions to your potential surrogate (regarding selective reduction and termination of the pregnancy); and (iii) coordinate various matters such as doctor appointments, transfer embryos from storage facilities to fertility clinics, and other issues.

TIP

Interviewing multiple surrogates may be necessary and finding the ideal surrogate is not always immediately accomplished. With open communication, time, and persistence, a perfect match can usually be found.

Some states have legal requirements for the qualifications of a surrogate (i.e., age); however, there are many practical and medical considerations to consider including whether she has her own children and experienced an uncomplicated birth, lives in a stable and healthy environment with supporting family/friends, and is free of any relevant or significant criminal history. A significant consideration when selecting a surrogate is to ensure that the surrogate is emotionally in agreement with the intended parents with regard to the issue of termination or selective reduction of the pregnancy in the event that too many embryos implant, as deemed safe by the attending physician, or there is a mental, physical, genetic or congenital defect, deformity, or disability with the child. It is important to understand that the intended parents cannot force a surrogate to terminate or not terminate a pregnancy. Therefore, it is critical for this topic to be discussed between the parties and with the licensed mental health professional to make sure everyone is on the same page.

Confirming or Obtaining Health Insurance

The intended parents are responsible to start the process of obtaining and confirming health insurance coverage for the surrogate as the maternity benefits are based on the surrogate's health insurance, if she has any. Insurance policies at times exclude surrogates to be eligible for coverage and subsequently ineligible for health insurance benefits. It is important to have the proper health insurance protection because intended parents are responsible for all health insurance costs for the surrogate relating to the pregnancy.

Insurance experts can be retained to review a surrogate's health insurance policy to determine whether any exclusion for surrogacy applies or to assist the intended parents in purchasing sufficient health insurance for the pregnancy. The process of reviewing a surrogate's health insurance benefits from the perspective of surrogacy insurance expert Marcie Maisonet with The Bayside Group (http://www.TheBaysideGroup.com) is as follows:

> Our first step, in the consultation process, is to determine if the surrogate carries an exclusion on a medical policy she may currently have in force.

It is very important to make certain there is no surrogacy exclusion. We require a certificate of coverage to be sent to us from the policyholder for review. If there is an exclusion, or if the surrogate carries no insurance, we will review all options for coverage to ensure that the proper policy is in place. The specific policy will cover the maternity care throughout the entire pregnancy. Once the policy is in force, a Confirmation of Coverage letter is mailed out to all parties involved.

The approximate timeframe to secure a policy is between thirty to forty-five days. The average monthly premium for the insurance policy will vary depending on the state you are residing in, and the age of the policyholder. Premiums can range anywhere from $275 monthly to $550 depending on the coverage and carrier of the policy. The insurance policy will be active for the entire pregnancy process, following two to three months after the birth. This will depend on whether a complication of pregnancy occurred and if the policy is still needed to cover the surrogate. All individual situations are different, and I recommend for each surrogacy, a consultation. There are many factors that would allow a surrogate to enroll in coverage, some during the open enrollment period, and some others may qualify throughout the year. It is best to speak with a surrogacy consultant who is knowledgeable and can assist with this process.

Determine Your Employer's Maternity Leave Policies

In anticipating taking off from work to deliver the child (surrogate) or to care for the child (intended parents), research your employer's maternity leave benefits to determine if the leave as a surrogate or intended parent is a paid leave (in accordance with your employer's employee guidelines), or whether you qualify under government-mandated unpaid leave requirements of the Family and Medical Leave Act, depending on your specific situation.

Select a Fertility Clinic

Simultaneously with the selection of a surrogate, the intended parents select the fertility clinic they wish to use to screen the surrogate and to create the embryos that will subsequently be transferred into the surrogate. It is important to confirm that the fertility clinic you've been working with also works with surrogates, as surrogacy requires specific federal guidelines, and not all fertility clinics offer this service to their patients. Based on the location of the surrogate, you may need to select a second fertility clinic, closer to the surrogate, to monitor her during the process to circumvent travel for routine appointments.

Egg, Sperm, or Embryo Donation Considerations

Additional considerations come into play when the intended parents utilize a genetic donor. Additional legal contracts, based upon the specific state laws involved, are required between the intended parents and donor (either with an anonymous or known donor) to protect the rights and obligations of all parties involved. Additional medical screening by the fertility clinic is also required of anyone donating genetic material.

Medically and Psychologically Clear the Surrogate

Once a match is made between a surrogate and intended parents, the surrogate has to clear a psychological analysis from a licensed mental health professional, and the surrogate has to be cleared medically by the reproductive physician to make sure she is fit to carry a child to term and is free of sexually transmitted diseases, among other medical considerations.

Finalize a Surrogacy Contract

Before fertility medications can start for the surrogate, a gestational surrogacy contract or similar type of agreement will be drafted, reviewed, and negotiated by the attorneys and then fully executed by the intended parents and surrogate (and spouse/partner, if applicable). The intended parents and the surrogate are represented by separate attorneys (both to be paid by the intended parents). It is critical to have the proper documentation in place with your surrogate prior to embarking upon the fertility procedures, in accordance with the appropriate state laws. Not to worry, however; your IVF clinic likely won't even let you proceed absent these crucial contracts.

Establish an Escrow Account

Prior to the embryo transfer and throughout the pregnancy, an escrow agent delivers the monies paid to the surrogate according to a schedule established in the contract. All funds are held in an independently managed escrow account so that the intended parents and surrogate do not have to exchange money during the surrogacy journey and all financial obligations are handled through the escrow agent to allow the intended parents and surrogate to focus on the pregnancy.

Medical Procedures

Once the embryos are created and the surrogate's uterus is at the right thickness, the embryos are transferred into the surrogate. The surrogate may then be required to stay off her feet for a period of time—perhaps a few days—to give the embryos the best shot at "sticking." The mantra you often hear repeated in the surrogacy world at this point in the process is "think sticky thoughts!" Following a wait of approximately two weeks (or the 2WW), the parties find out whether or not the surrogate is pregnant.

Graduate from Fertility Clinic to Obstetrician

The surrogate will continue to see the fertility doctor until around eight to ten weeks of pregnancy. She is then released to an obstetrician, to be selected by the parties and based on the surrogate's insurance. Fertility medications for the surrogate may continue for up to twelve weeks of pregnancy, depending on the opinion of the fertility doctor.

Depending on the terms of the surrogacy contract, the intended parents may be permitted to attend all obstetrician and gynecologist (OB/GYN) appointments and obtain any medical information, tests, or records relating to the surrogate's

OB/GYN care for the pregnancy. You may consider having the intended parents call the OB/GYN's office before the surrogate starts her care to enlighten them of the surrogacy arrangement to make sure the staff is aware of the all of the parties involved and that the intended parents have full rights to information following each visit. This is absolutely routine, so if your surrogate's OB office treats this as an unusual situation or gives you any kind of a hard time, they just don't "get it" and are probably inexperienced as to surrogacy. Your lawyer may have to intervene if you are not receiving the treatment and/or information to which you are entitled by virtue of the surrogate's wishes and her executed release of medical information (a/k/a "HIPAA form").

Coordinate Birth Plan with Hospital

It is important for the hospital staff to understand the surrogacy arrangement so the intended parents have full hospital access to the child. Many hospitals formulate a birth plan between the parties, which includes who has access to the nursery, whether the intended parents want a separate room for visitation, and who has access to the delivery room in the event of a vaginal birth or cesarean section. Once again, the hospital administration ought to understand the surrogacy arrangement and honor the parties'

CAUTION Hospital employees, doctors, doctor office employees, nurses—these are all human beings with their own backgrounds and perspectives. As much as they are discouraged to do so, they may bring their personal agendas to work with them.

wishes. This is supposed to be an anxious but happy time! If any hospital employee or administrator is interfering with the plan as expressed by the parties, the next person up the food chain in the hospital's chain of command should be notified, and the lawyer could be brought in if necessary.

Somewhere along the line of your surrogacy journey you may find someone—a relative, coworker, or friend—who just doesn't believe in what you're doing. Oftentimes these feelings come from a religious belief that you're "playing God." Try as they may, these people may be unable to shake their personal judgments as to your ART journey.

When these people are hospital nurses, it gets considerably more uncomfortable. What should be a happy time for the surrogate, intended parents, and other family members can feel dirty and uncomfortable and sometimes worse.

Get Trust and Estate Documents in Order for the Intended Parents

When contemplating building a family, we recommend getting the right legal documents in place to make sure that the gestating child is protected in case something happens to the intended parents either during the pregnancy or after the child is born. Language to this effect ought to exist in the surrogacy contract, but it wouldn't hurt at all to ask your lawyer to refer you to a colleague who is proficient at preparing wills and trusts, and other instruments that will help to protect your family's financial future. The procurement of life insurance for the surrogate has already been done, but how about for the intended parents? These are considerations that ought to be discussed in the early stages.

Prepare for Baby

Even though the intended mother is not carrying her child, there are still many things to do to prepare for the baby's arrival: furnish and decorate the nursery, purchase the baby gear and accessories, babyproof the house, and all the other fun things that come along with getting ready to bring a baby into your home.

Intended parents may want to consider taking parenting classes at their local hospital such as baby care, safety, or infant CPR. Brace yourself that the intended mother will be in the company of all pregnant women in these settings and emotionally, this may be difficult. Just know that you are just as much of as an expectant mother as the rest of the women and deserve to be in that class too!

If you feel comfortable, consider having a gender reveal and/or baby shower to celebrate this wonderful experience and even get some great gifts to help you prepare for the big day.

When thinking about having a child, it is essential to consider—what if your child has special needs of some kind? There is no indication that ART results in special needs children at any higher likelihood than any other method of family creation, including the old-fashioned way. (The exception to this would be ART twin pregnancies, which carry a higher risk but only because of the higher risk nature of multiple pregnancies . . . nothing to do with the ART itself.) With that said, there is still the chance that your child/ren will be born with or will develop some type of issue that would necessitate atypical care.

Coauthor Jeff Kasky's third child, which was the product of a "normal" and healthy pregnancy, was born with autism. How? Why? Who knows? But however or whyever, there are extraordinary lifetime expenses involved in taking care of that person, above and beyond what would have been involved in raising a so-called neurotypical person.

The purpose of raising this issue is to a) get you to consider how you would handle the additional expenses that come along with this territory, and b) get you thinking about this early, so in the unlikely event it happens it's not a blindside.

There's always a light at the end of the tunnel. Coauthor Kasky was inspired by his son's condition and saw the need to provide information and entertainment within the autism community. He is now the president of The Autism Channel (http://www.theautismchannel.tv)!

Establishing Parental Rights of Intended Parents

Either before or after the child is born, the procedures making sure the surrogate's name is not on the birth certificate and placing the intended parents' names on the birth certificate is a matter of state law. It is critical that intended parents consult with an experienced ART attorney at the beginning of the process so they understand the procedures and risks, if any, based on that particular state's laws and regulations on surrogacy. For international parents using a surrogate in the

United States, one must discuss immigration issues to ensure that the child, who is be issued a birth certificate in the state of birth, is able to reenter the international intended parents' home country and obtain citizenship, as each country has different regulations and procedures for this process.

Suffice it to say that losing or even having to fight for your child is the worst nightmare a parent can face. If the legal rights to a child are not clear, the courts will create them as best they can to protect that child. If surrogacy, or any form of parenting for that matter, is not done in the way that creates the correct rights in the intended parties, you're asking for that nightmare. That's why is so important to proceed with an experienced advocate.

Breast Milk for the Child

Got milk? The surrogate postbirth most likely does! Many surrogates are willing to pump their breast milk for the child following delivery. The intended parents usually pay either a weekly or monthly fee for the milk, along with all the expenses required to pump the milk such as the breast pump, milk bags, and any shipping required. Many times the fees associated with breast milk are contemplated in the surrogacy contract.

Some intended mothers are able to provide their own breast milk for the child under the supervision and medical direction of a physician; typically a cocktail of hormones is required for the intended mother to produce milk.

Using a Surrogacy Agency

The surrogacy process can be overwhelming, but with the right team in place, it can be a beautiful way to build a family.

Most of the players involved in the process, which includes attorneys, physicians, mental health professionals, are all licensed professionals who report to a strict higher governing authority and are subject to state disciplinary bodies for violating both standards of practice and ethical rules. However, some of the critical players, such as surrogacy and egg donor agencies, that help locate and handle the logistics of the process operate with little to no regulation. Currently, anyone can open a surrogacy agency, and the laws do not provide any guidelines or require agencies to run criminal background checks or have a surrogacy agency license.

Similar to picking players on a successful sports team, when using a surrogate, you want to make sure you "draft" the right team members.

While there are many incredible surrogacy and egg donor agencies that do provide invaluable service to clients, there is also a history of incompetent and even intentional fraud and criminal practices that have occurred that has led to extreme frustration, emotional distress, and financial loss. An example of a surrogacy agency gone wrong was seen with a California surrogacy lawyer and owner of Conceptual Options, who was convicted in a baby-selling ring.

The baby-selling ring solicited surrogates online to carry children for fictitious intended parents and sent the surrogates to Ukraine to have embryos transferred without having intended parents ready to accept the child. Once the surrogate was well into the pregnancy, representatives of this agency would tell the surrogates that the (fictitious) parents had "backed out," and would then sell the babies for more than $100,000 apiece.

Benefits of a Surrogacy Agency

A good surrogacy agency not only locates surrogates (either within the state of the intended parents or possibly from around the country) but also acts as a facilitator for the entire surrogacy process. This can and often will result in the relief of an extraordinary amount of stress and confusion for all parties.

An agency can locate a prescreened egg donor and surrogate, perform home assessments of the surrogate, provide guidance of the expenses associated with the process, recommend reputable professionals to assist with the psychological screening, medical procedures, and legal team, and continue to play a role supporting the relationship between the intended parents and the surrogate— through thick and thin. When trying to find a surrogate solo, you may not know the red flags to look for in picking a surrogate or where to even find someone to act as a surrogate. Experienced agencies and facilitators have heard all the stories and know the red flags when they see them. This can save you time, expense, and heartache way above and beyond the actual cost of the agency's fee.

An invaluable contribution of a surrogacy agency is that they act as a middleman between the intended parents and the surrogate. The relationship between the parties is part business deal and part an emotionally charged endeavor. Discussing financials and business terms between the intended parents and the surrogate can be uncomfortable and even lead to negative dealings between the parties. This should be avoided however reasonably possible. When working with a surrogacy agency, the agency should negotiate all of the expenses paid to the surrogate so that the intended parents and surrogate never have to discuss money issues. This keeps the relationship between the intended parents and surrogate focused on the end goal of a healthy pregnancy, without muddying the waters with financial negotiation.

How to Select a Reputable Surrogacy Agency

Anyone can open up shop and call themselves a surrogacy agency. So with no regulation over this form of business, how does one know what to look for in a reputable surrogacy agency? There are numerous agency options to choose from, and it is imperative to select a company that actually knows what they are doing. That being said, for someone new to the surrogacy world, it is hard to know whom to trust. Every surrogacy agency functions a little differently, including how much they charge for an agency fee, rematch or refund matters, and how much they suggest for the compensation to the surrogate, so you have to do your homework when picking an agency that works for you. A good starting point is to ask questions.

Your best resource may be word-of-mouth from friends, acquaintances, or others who have gone through the process. When either searching for or doing your research on a particular agency, you can:

1. Ask any former intended parents, surrogates, or donors for an agency recommendation.
2. Ask your fertility clinic or a local fertility clinic for a recommendation.
3. Search the agency on the Internet and on fertility blogs. While you can't trust everything you read on the Internet, you should obviously be cautious if you read a lot of bad reviews about an agency.
4. Check your state's department of consumer affairs, or similar department, to check for business complaints.
5. Check if the agency is registered on the agency's state's Secretary of State to ensure it is a valid business in good standing with the state it practices in.

Questions Directed to the Agency

1. Does the agency have a physical office at which meetings can be held?
2. How long has the agency been in business?
3. How many clients has the agency guided through the process?
4. How long does it take to get matched with a surrogate?
5. What type of screening does the agency perform when selecting a surrogate (i.e., do they perform home study, psychological analysis, background check, etc.)?
6. Ask to review the surrogacy agency contract to make sure you feel comfortable with the terms (i.e., make sure any required deposits seem reasonable for the work which they are performing) or have it reviewed by an attorney.
7. Ask how much the agency charges for their services and how it is paid (e.g., paid in installments as the matching process progresses).
8. Does the agency attend the ASRM conferences and perform continued learning of the ART world?
9. Does the agency provide a comprehensive case manager as a point person to talk to during the process for any questions or concerns?

Surrogate Matching Process

Each agency works differently, but generally, in order for a surrogate to be properly screened by an agency, the surrogate starts by completing an application with the agency. The surrogate must provide all of her prior medical records relating to her previous pregnancies. Also, if a surrogate has acted as a surrogate before, she should provide her prior IVF cycle records and information on the previous delivery. The potential surrogate should also provide her Pap smear, current within the past twelve months. The surrogacy agency will initially review these medical records, at times with an on-staff medical professional. A surrogate should also provide the surrogacy agency with a copy of her medical insurance benefits (if she has health insurance coverage), along with copies of her most recent paystubs. This will allow the agency to make a cursory review of the medical insurance to determine if she has medical coverage for surrogacy and to determine how much income the surrogate makes so that when it is time to match her with the intended parents, the intended parents will know how much they will need to pay in lost wages if the surrogate misses work due to an issue with the pregnancy.

Once a surrogate joins an agency's program, she then gets matched with the intended parents. Typically the first step is to share the surrogate's profile with the intended parents to make an initial determination if the surrogate is a good fit. The surrogacy agency requests that any potential intended parent complete a profile revealing their background information so they are properly matched. If the intended parents like the profile, the parties may have a telephone call or video conference to become acquainted with one another. If that meeting is successful, the parties will arrange to meet in person. A representative from the agency attends and facilitates the conversation at these meetings, as it may be an awkward situation for these strangers to meet to discuss such an important journey. While the issue of selective reduction and termination is further discussed during the psychological review and with the attorneys, the agency's representative guides the parties to discuss the topic of whether or not the parties are on the same page in this realm, in the event something is wrong with the fetus or if there are more than two embryos that implant in the surrogate's uterus.

Self-Matching with a Surrogate through Friends and Family

Some people do not use an agency to find a surrogate for various reasons. The intended parents may have a friend or family member willing to carry for them, or they may not be able to afford an agency fee and have to locate a surrogate on their own.

When looking for a surrogate without the use of an agency, infertility advocate, former intended mother, and infertility blogger (http://www.whitneyanderick.com) Whitney Anderson writes the following advice from her blog:

1. Tell everyone you know! Share this with friends and family on a one-on-one basis as you see people. Share your story and your interest in pursuing surrogacy and ask if they know of anyone. This will also serve to ask them indirectly as well. If people don't know you are infertile, if they don't know your story, if they don't know you are specifically looking for a surrogate, how on earth would they offer to help or connect you with the right person? The more information, the better. People really do want to help. They will emotionally connect with your story and will want to help you if only to share your story. IF YOU DO NOTHING ELSE, THIS WOULD BE THE MOST IMPORTANT! If you can't do this, which is fine, you really might have to consider using an agency instead. Most intended parents [whom] I know end up using a family member, a friend, or a friend of a friend. They got the word out and someone volunteered. This is where the luck [part] comes in. We aren't all that lucky. If not, keep reading.

2. Make sure your clinic knows of your interest in this as well. Hopefully, you've already talked to them about it. Ask them if they know of anyone interested.

3. Call around to area churches and speak to the pastors and tell them you are interested in pursuing this and see if they know of anyone.

4. Post about it on social media. This requires you to be open about it, but if you want to find a surrogate on your own, you will have to break out of your comfort zone.

5. Set up a Google alert for surrogacy and check out articles in major news-papers, magazines, or websites published online regarding surrogacy. If it allows comments, say that you are looking for a surrogate and share your URL or email. A friend did this for me, and I was contacted by seven women right after she did that. They were all over the country and who knows how serious they were, but it opened a lot of doors. We didn't pursue any of these people, because we were already pursuing things with Nicole.

6. Consider creating a website—use wordpress.com, which is free and easy. Use this to market yourselves to potential surrogates. We created a web-site to market ourselves for potential surrogates and adoption matches.

7. Create a Facebook page and ask friends/family to share—we had 300 likes in 3 days. (A bunch of strangers liked our page, which was perfect because it expanded our reach.)

8. Make a pitch to your local media—TV, magazines, and newspapers. Share your infertility story and tell them you need their help to find the perfect person.

9. Join my Surrogacy Meet-up group on Facebook that I created to help intended parents and gestational carriers find one another. No promises, just trying to help. Also, search for other Facebook groups on surrogacy.

10. Surrogacy Forums—there are several, and I checked them out but never felt right about using them. Seemed so spammy or just people looking to make money. Not only could we not afford a high rate, but we didn't want someone who was only doing it for the money. I just never could get into these websites.

Considerations When Surrogate Is a Friend or Family Member

Pregnancy can be a dangerous prospect. A woman can lose her reproductive or-gans rendering her unable to have more children and it may even result in death. While these situations are unlikely, you have to consider . . . how would you feel if your sister was your surrogate and something horrible happened to her? There are additional factors you have to take into account when asking someone you know well to act as your surrogate.

While there may be some obvious advantages to having friends or family act as a surrogate, including a higher level of trust and possibly saving on expenses, such benefits do not come without additional risks and unique considerations. Questions raised by the ASRM as it relates to first-degree family members acting as surrogates include: "Can a donor or surrogate closely tied to and perhaps dependent on the re-cipient couple make a free and fully informed decision? What are the consequences

Jeannette Ziobro of Life Through Surrogacy, Inc. (http://www.lifethroughsurrogacy.com) reports that approximately eight out of every ten women who apply to be a surrogate do not qualify for one reason or another. The top disqualifying factors are BMI (height/weight ratio), the applicant does not have the required childbirth history, and the applicant does not have the "roots in the community" stability that Jeannette is looking for. Women who volunteer to carry for you are offering to do something tremendous and wonderful. However, when push comes to shove, they oftentimes either don't qualify medically and emotionally or don't follow through when they realize all that's involved.

NOTE

of the unusual resulting relationships on the donor or surrogate, donor-conceived persons, and rest of the family?"[5] Additional concerns raised by the ASRM include, What if the IVF is not successful, how will this impact the parties' relationship? What if the child is born with a genetic or birth defect, how will that impact the parties' relationship? Will the surrogate have problems detaching herself from the child since the child will be in her life more than may be with an unfamiliar surrogate? Many of these questions are answered in a different way depending on the physical and emotional closeness of the parties, the maturity of the families involved, and other factors such as financial dependency.

Whenever considering using a family member or friend as a surrogate, it is crucial that all parties discuss the following: (i) emotional implications involved with a licensed mental health professional (this therapy should include the intended parents, the surrogate and her spouse/partner, and possibly other immediate family members and the future children when they are older); (ii) physical implications involved with a licensed medical professional to address the medical risks involved, including the medications used with ART and risks of ART and pregnancy; and (iii) legal implications involved with an ART attorney in the applicable state to ensure that the parties legal parenting rights are protected and properly explained.

There are competing arguments as far as whether and to what extent the government should be involved in your personal life, including the decisions you make about reproduction and how you go about achieving your family plan. Certainly some regulation should be in place, as it is, to protect the public from disease and physical, legal, and emotional catastrophe. However, should there be legal qualifications as to what criteria a woman must meet in order to be considered for surrogacy? Further, as discussed more fully herein, surrogacy agencies and similar entities are, for the most part, not licensed or regulated. This means you should tread very carefully and do the most research you can before engaging anyone to help you for payment.

What to Look for in a Surrogate

Once again, you have to know your specific state law to determine if there are any legal requirements of a surrogate. Some states require the surrogate to be within

[5] https://www.asrm.org/uploadedFiles/ASRM_Content/News_and_Publications/Ethics_Committee_Reports_and_Statements/family_members.pdf.

a certain age group, to have had a prior live birth, or do not allow a surrogate to receive any form of compensation.

What to Look for in a Surrogate: Fertility Doctor's Perspective

Dr. Mark Denker, reproductive physician, opines on some of the qualifications medically speaking when he evaluates a potential surrogate:

> The selection and screening of gestational surrogates has changed over the years. Initially, surrogates were required to be in excellent physical health, not be overweight, and to pass psychological exams and interviews. In addition, to qualify as a surrogate, women were not permitted more than three cesarean sections, four vaginal deliveries, or some combination thereof. With the increasing popularity of gestational surrogacy, however, the pool of available surrogates has diminished, necessitating a wider net be cast in order to allow enough surrogates into the screening process to accommodate the demand. Historical requirements for a maximum body mass index (BMI), age, or number of cesarean sections have basically disappeared from the surrogate-screening landscape. Currently, it is not unusual to accept a surrogate that has had six pregnancies, four or more C-sections, and is overweight. In these situations in particular, it is advisable to obtain prior assessment and clearance from a maternal-fetal medicine specialist.

What to Look for from a Surrogate–Surrogacy Agent's Perspective

Jeannette Ziobro, former surrogate and president of surrogacy agency Life Through Surrogacy (http://www.lifethroughsurrogacy.com), provides her experience successfully matching intended parents with a surrogate and what she looks for in her expert opinion when selecting a surrogate:

> Carrying a baby for someone who cannot is an extraordinarily unselfish act. The fact that the gestational carrier is reimbursed for her living expenses—or even compensated in some way—does not take away from the beauty or selflessness of thee act. As a person who has been pregnant with and delivered twins I can tell you from firsthand experience—if you're doing it for the money alone, it's just not worth it!
>
> As the president of a Florida surrogacy agency I am oftentimes recruiting prospective surrogates to carry for the agency's clients. I estimate that fewer than 20 percent of the women who go so far as to apply to become a surrogate actually pass through the process and are matched with a prospective intended family. The categories through which each prospective surrogate must clear, not necessarily in order of importance, are medical, psychological, and mine.

Medical

A mathematician named Lambert Adolphe Jacques Quetelet in the nineteenth century came up with a system through which a person's BMI can be calculated. Some find the system fairly crude and rudimentary, as it only looks at sex, height, and weight. There is no calculation involving how much of one's weight is fat versus muscle, or whether the weight can be accounted for in one area or another on one's body. For example, a woman who is 5'1" tall and weighs 140 lbs. has a BMI of 26. The fact that her waist might be usually proportioned but her butt or breasts carry more than usual weight is not factored in.

A healthy BMI is considered 18.5—24.9. This means that a man who is 6' tall cannot weigh over 180 or he is considered overweight. If that man weighs 181 he is considered obese! A woman of average height, such as 5'5", must weigh no more than 150 to be considered within a "normal" BMI. She is considered overweight at 160 and obese at 190.

Many infertility doctors will not work with prospective gestational carriers who don't fall within the healthy BMI range of 19–27. Some doctors are slightly less conservative insofar as agreeing to work with women whose BMIs fall into the "overweight" category but are otherwise healthy. BMI is the most likely criterion through which a prospective surrogate will fall out of eligibility.

A prospective surrogate is given a very thorough health assessment as part of the qualifying process. Her blood pressure is taken. She is tested for alcohol and drug use and is screened for sexually transmitted diseases, vitamin levels, and thyroid levels. Her partner is also tested.

A prospective surrogate's uterus is carefully examined for any cysts, fibroids, or fluid pockets, which may interfere with the transfer or implantation of the embryo(s). She is carefully explored inside and out to assure that her body is in the peak condition for accepting and carrying a pregnancy. Anything anomalous will likely rule her out of eligibility as a surrogate.

Psychological

A prospective surrogate's psychological soundness is crucial to the surrogacy process. She must be willing and able to go through what is a rigorous process of medications, suppositories, and injections to prepare her body for the transfer and the pregnancy. She is completely responsible for taking her medications as and when directed. Once pregnant, she is responsible for living a healthy lifestyle supportive of and consistent with pregnancy. She has to avoid many activities that she would otherwise be free to do. She agrees to forego hair treatments, nail treatments, certain medications, participation in sports, and third-trimester travel, among others. The psychological clearance seeks to confirm that the gestational carrier in question can make such sacrifices for a year and that her spouse or partner, children, and other supportive personnel are there to help her.

The psych clearance also seeks to confirm that the prospective surrogate can and will form only a healthy attachment to the child whom she is carrying and will not suffer undue psychological distress when handing the child over to the parent(s). Further concern is given to the surrogate's own child(ren), who have to be made to understand at some point in the process that mommy is pregnant but that the baby belongs to someone else, and mommy is doing a very nice thing by taking care of the baby while the other mommy is unable. (The foregoing is only an example, of course. Prospective intended parents do not always involve a mommy.)

The psychological exam usually includes the Minnesota Multiphasic Personality Inventory, also known as the MMPI. The MMPI is an exhausting test comprised of yes/no, true/false questions of a repetitive and often confusing nature. That test is often accompanied by an interview with the therapist who is administering the psychological screening. Sometimes the surrogate is interviewed alone, and sometimes the interview is conducted with her partner (if any). Sometimes the prospective intended family is also interviewed with the prospective surrogate. Ultimately, clearance is sought for the surrogate and the family to move forward in the process.

This psychological clearance process is yet another layer of protection that all parties can use. The surrogate knows that she's bringing a child into a loving and capable home, and the intended parents know the woman who is carrying their child is unlikely to suffer any emotional trauma and is further unlikely to do anything during the pregnancy that may be inconsistent with a healthy pregnancy.

Surrogacy Agent's Personal Perspective

I will not agree to work with a prospective surrogate, no matter how physically and psychologically healthy she is, if I would not want her to carry my very own baby for me. Further, if a woman seems overly high maintenance (constant and unrelenting calls, texts, and emails, particularly during nonbusiness hours for nonemergency issues), I would not want to match her with a family lest she demand an unreasonable amount of attention and thus create a situation wherein the intended parents cringe every time the phone rings. It is usually very obvious from the outset as to who the prima donnas are, and they will likely not get past the first couple of phone calls with me.

In my subjective but experienced opinion, and having been a surrogate myself, I believe that the best candidate for the very important role as gestational carrier, from a personality and stability perspective, has some or most of the following attributes:

- She is a good and responsible parent.
- She has a regular job or a partner who does.
- She has a supportive partner.
- She is stable, with well-established roots in the community.
- She laughs and rolls her eyes when asked if she uses illegal drugs, as if to say "if you only knew me you would never ask that question!".
- She is looking forward to helping people and views the money involved as an extra added bonus, not the driving force for the decision.
- She keeps appointments for phone calls with me, doctors, and lawyers involved in the case and, of course, prospective intended parents.
- She has a regular OB and is known and liked by the practice.
- She asks good questions and signs paperwork only after reading it.

Surrogacy from the Eyes of a Surrogate

Coauthor Marla B. Neufeld's surrogate Caitlin beautifully shares her positive experience acting as surrogate. She highlights some challenges and provides insight into some emotional considerations when acting as a surrogate:

I was first introduced to surrogacy at a young age. My mother always talked about it and wanted to be one for my cousin. She never had the honor of being his. So when I met with the woman who would help change my life and someone else's forever, my first thought was, do it for Mom. Do it in her memory and in honor for her. That's what really made my final decision in becoming a surrogate. Then after hearing the pain and suffering this couple had been going through for the past three years, it hurt my heart. Hearing that a couple who was happily married, both had amazing careers, had made a life for themselves and the only missing piece to their puzzle was not able happening for·them. Right then I knew, I was the one for them. The one that would be help them become parents.

When I first heard about the whole process of the IVF treatment, I was a little nervous. I have never really had to take shots or hormone medicines ever before. Luckily I have a great support system at home and we all were in for a wild ride. Taking the hormone shots were OK, uncomfortable, but I managed. Not knowing how my body was going to change was a surprise. Morning sickness, ten times worse. Being tired all the time, ten times worse. Having to go to multiple doctors' appointments, blood work after blood work, shot after shot. I would have to say that was the hardest part of the whole surrogate process. My friends and family thought I was crazy, not because I was a surrogate, but because the hormones made me extremely moody. Then when the doctor finally said, "Caitlin, you are ready to go," and I was on a jet plane down to Miami. I finely met the couple I would be surrogating for. Marla and Jason. I stayed with them, and they took care of me while I was down for the transfer. Marla stayed with me, by my side, for the whole entire process. A woman, I had only met the day before, held my hand and sat in the room next to me while the fertility doctor transferred her embryos into my uterus (which I was told by every doctor that it was beautiful). We laughed and cried, watching the sonogram of the embryos going in and about thirty minutes after laying, with my whole body tilted, we were ready to go home. I stayed at Marla and Jason's house for about three days on strict bed rest. In doing so, I got to meet their lovely family and try new foods I never had before, quinoa and Thai takeout. I was also introduced to *Orange is the New Black*, which by the way is my favorite show now. After then, going back to my home in Orlando, within a few days, I took a pregnancy test and called Miss Marla and Mr. Jason to tell them that I was pregnant.

Over the next nine months, I carried twin boys and at the end, I had a C-section, giving life to two beautiful little bundles of joy. Some people ask me, "How can you give the babies up?" or "You're not attached?" and my answer was always the same. Of course I was attached, I carried these boys for nine months and made sure they were growing and healthy. Any human would be attached; it's nature. The fact that I was helping someone in a way I have never helped before, giving them last hope for biological children. Seeing Marla and Jason's face when the found out they were having boys, seeing them get excited about buying car seats and diaper bags, hearing them tear up as we discussed how I was feeling them kick and move. All the things I experienced was worth every moment, seeing them happy. I looked at it as I was their first real babysitter, and they were my "womb" mates. I took care of them, helped them grow, fed them, stayed up all hours of the night with them, but then when it was time for them to go home, they did, and I was okay with that. Being witness to a mother and father, who had already been through so much, hold their boys for the first time. Seeing them feed them, change them for the first time, priceless! Having this moment added to my life is just as big as when I had my own children. We are all here for a reason; we all have a plan set in motion every day. We are on this earth to help one another out in time of need. That's what I did, and I am happy to say I will be doing it again. Setting an example for my children to follow. Letting them know, it's okay to help people, to be there for someone you barely know, it's okay. Give it your all, and put 100 percent of you into everything you do. One day you might need help in return, and the reward in doing so is life changing. Teamwork makes the dream work.

Surrogacy vs. Adoption

Never before have two processes with such a similar outcome been so very different.

For the purpose of the rest of this section, we are describing the most commonly considered variety of surrogacy—gestational surrogacy—with the type of adoption that is most likely what comes to mind when thinking about or discussing adoption—the private adoption wherein a birth mother places a baby for permanent adoption through a lawyer or agency. (Statistically speaking, there are far more step-parent adoptions and interfamily adoptions than the private variety that we discuss herein, but for those who are suffering from infertility, "adoption" usually refers to the private variety.) We acknowledge that there are a variety of types of surrogacy and adoption and that the facts as listed below are mere generalizations. However, we also feel that with our experience in having done both for many, many years, we have earned the right to make these generalizations, because politically correct or not, they are accurate in many if not most cases. Furthermore, you already know by now that surrogacy and adoption are regulated by state laws and thus the rules are different from state-to-state. The following generalizations about the process may not be 100 percent accurate for each and every state, so, once again, consult a lawyer!

Surrogacy is the process wherein a clean, healthy, and carefully vetted woman volunteers, out of the goodness of her heart (and probably also a desire to supplement her income) to carry a pregnancy for a person or couple whom she has met and approved. Adoption takes many forms, but the subcategory that is often being considered is the type wherein a pregnant woman is, for any number of reasons, considers placing her as-yet-unborn child for permanent adoption.

Prior to the beginning of the process and certainly before a pregnancy, a surrogate is explored carefully from a personal perspective (meetings and visits); a medical perspective (numerous tests and medical appointments); a social perspective (subjective judgment as to her ability to follow through with the entire process and her stability and ties to the community); a legal perspective (lawyers are involved!); and a psychological perspective (meetings with a therapist including counseling and testing). By contrast, a birth mother is pregnant already, and the pregnancy was almost always unexpected and sometimes "unwanted." A surrogate is legally able to receive financial payments, sometimes called "compensation," for her time, effort, discomfort, and for the service that she's providing. A birth mother is not. In neither case is it ever legal or moral or proper to "sell a baby." In the case of a gestational surrogate, the baby has always belonged, in every way possible, to the intended parents. Thus, the financial assistance or compensation she receives is for her expenses, pain and suffering, extraordinary efforts, etc. By contrast, a birth mother is the "owner" of the baby that she is carrying and has the parental rights as such. Financial assistance to her must be for her reasonable expenses only, and in no way can it be used as compensation in exchange for her baby!

A surrogate is a person with some stability and social connection to the community. She may own a house and have a good job where she has established herself within the organization. She may have family close by, kids in area schools, a spouse or partner with a good job. A good candidate for surrogacy will lead a fairly uneventful life, free of any major conflict or excitement.

By contrast, a birth mother is a person who is typically in crisis for the majority of her day, week, month, year, and life. She is being evicted. She is in jail, again. Her boyfriend was just arrested, again. She missed her last three doctor appointments because she knows she's going to be drug tested. At her first appointment, she got mad and "cussed out" the doctor because he told her she should cut down on the pack-a-day smoking habit, which she can somehow afford despite her poverty. She smoked with her last three kids and they're fine, and she doesn't see how it's any of the doctor's business. She has had her kids taken away from her by the Department of Children and Family Services; she may or may not ever see them again. She sometimes has to resort to turning tricks to get money for pills so she doesn't get dope sick. She hasn't eaten in three days. Her phone was turned off because she forgot to tell the agency to pay the bill. Her purse was stolen on the bus, right after she cashed her grocery money assistance check . . . again.

In surrogacy there is a contract in place outlining the rights, responsibilities, and expectations of all of the parties. Thus there are very few, if any, surprises. In adoption if a contract exists, it is probably just to outline the hopes of how the process will play out, but it likely has no legal import at all. Financially, many adoptions are a loosely regulated free-for-all, and the final cost of an adoption is often different from the initial projection. This is mainly due to the instability of the birth parent(s)' living situation.

The gestational surrogate has absolutely no legal right to the child. At the end of the pregnancy, there is no question whatsoever that the baby should be physically given directly to his parent(s), and it is their decision as to whether to share that time with the surrogate. There is some postdelivery paperwork, and there are may be some legal proceedings, but they should be perfunctory insofar as they simply serve to acknowledge what we have always known—that these parents are the legal parents of this child, despite the fact that the child was birthed by the surrogate.

The birth mother is the legal and biological mother of the child born to her pregnancy. She can decide to complete the adoption if she wants, or she can cancel her adoption plan, despite having been supported financially by the agency and/or family. The birth mother will be presented with the paperwork that she can sign to voluntarily, permanently, and hopefully irrevocably terminate her parental rights to the child. She may have a period of time after that paperwork is signed during which she can actually revoke her consent and keep the baby, for any reason or for no reason at all. The birth mother can pick up the phone in the hospital room, call the nurses' station, and have the hospital exclude the prospective adoptive family and their representatives/attorneys from the building. It is not unheard of at all for the birth mother, knowing these rights, to make a last-minute effort to "negotiate" a new postdelivery support arrangement, using the baby as her bargaining chip.

In surrogacy, the main area of risk is whether the IVF procedures will result in a pregnancy. The risk of the surrogate disappearing, using drugs or alcohol, or otherwise creating a legal situation exists, but the vetting process—including the psychological counseling—is designed to come as close as possible to eliminating such issues. Most surrogacies are fairly unexciting.

In adoption, the myriad risks include whether the birth mother will damage the fetus/baby with bad lifestyle choices during the pregnancy, whether she is scamming by pretending she's going to place the baby just so she can take financial support, and whether she is going to have a genuine change of heart at the end and keep the baby or give it to a friend or family member. We haven't even mentioned the concerns relating to the birth father!

The choice between adoption versus surrogacy boils down to several considerations:

1. The adoption agency's/lawyer's waiting list and whether you are willing to wait for what could be years and could be a week.
2. Your allocation of financial and emotional risk, as described above.
3. Your ability to understand and tolerate lifestyle issues, sometimes including substance abuse, being practiced by the woman carrying the child, whom you hope will someday be yours.

Coauthor Jeff Kasky, who has been handling private adoptions for over twenty years, says this: "I do not have what it takes emotionally to handle the process of private adoption, some cases of which can be compared to riding a roller-coaster whilst blindfolded, on PCP through a sharknado in the deepest depths of hell itself, all while throwing fists full of hundred dollar bills into the top of a volcano."

CHAPTER

6

International ART: Crossing the Sea to Start a Family

Considerations with International ART

Introduction to Cross-Border Reproductive Care or Fertility Tourism

Cross-border reproductive care, also referred to as *fertility tourism*, is the concept of travelling from your home state to either another state or country to receive reproductive treatment and services.

This concept is becoming increasingly popular for a variety of reasons, which chiefly include the possibility of:

- Better quality of medical care and more specialized services in the destination country;
- Lower costs for fertility treatment, which may include IVF, surrogacy, or egg donation;
- Avoiding certain legal complications or barriers in the home state (i.e., if surrogacy is illegal in home state or if home state restricts medical services, such as certain genetic testing or controversial medical procedures);
- Maintaining a patient's privacy or level of familiarity in the destination country;
- Avoiding a long wait time for services such as locating a surrogate or donor.

Considerations when Traveling Abroad for ART

Think of all the things you have to plan when travelling for vacation. While travelling is glamorous and exciting, it can be difficult. There is a reason Al Gore once said, "Airplane travel is nature's way of making you look like your passport photo." Now add to the travelling logistics everything you will need to consider relating to the ART procedures, which includes medical, legal and psychological components. When traveling, especially travelling abroad, there are many considerations to take into account to make sure the ART process is smooth and successful. While saving money is great, it is important to consider various factors to ensure the savings do not compromise your ART experience. While the below considerations are important when travelling between states for ART, the implications are greater and worth bearing in mind when travelling abroad internationally for ART treatment and services.

Safety and Health

In the United States, the medical procedures for ART are highly regulated and controlled, especially when it comes to preventing the transmission of infectious diseases or genetic disorders. Since there is no international policy or laws about quality control measures and standard of care for ART patients traveling abroad, it is important to make sure the proper precautions are taken in the destination fertility clinic.

Language Barriers

When travelling internationally for vacation purposes it is a challenge just to find out where the bathroom is at a restaurant. Now consider not knowing a foreign language and having figure out the medical practices and guidelines of a fertility clinic. Along with further distances from home come challenges to language barriers and difficulty obtaining accurate and understandable information on medical procedures, instructions, and valid informed consents.

Emotional Challenges

Some fertility facilities abroad have excellent quality of care for the patients and surrogates; however, some facilities, specifically surrogacy and donation centers abroad, may have questionable practices as to how they treat their surrogate and egg donors. Poor treatment of surrogate and donors abroad may inflict physical, social, and psychological harm to such donors and surrogates that may impact the ART experience for all parties involved, to say the very least.

Economic Challenges

On paper, ART procedures may be less expensive abroad, but you have to consider the big picture when formulating a budget. Traveling is expensive. When considering going abroad for ART treatment, you have to factor into your budget expenses that may not be incurred if the procedures are done locally, such as airfare, hotels, meals, transportation, the possible shipment of embryos, increased legal fees for immigration purposes, postdelivery hospitalization of the child, and the inevitable "surprise" charges, costs, and expenses that invariably arise. Additionally, intended parents going abroad are suggested to factor in multiple visits to the destination country and staying in the destination country for as long as thirty to forty-five days, depending on type of procedures involved, which is an expensive endeavor and difficult for many people to miss work for that amount of time.

Legal Implications

We don't just say this because we are lawyers but perhaps the most vexing considerations with fertility tourism are the legal considerations. There are numerous legal variables that need to be factored in when using fertility tourism. You have left the United States to use an egg donor and surrogate in a foreign country, and the child is born abroad. What is the citizenship of that child? Will they be able to return to the United States as a US citizen? What happens if customs does not permit you to leave the foreign country with the child? Being in a foreign country, it may be difficult to obtain legal advice and legal remedies.

When doing your homework on traveling abroad for ART services, consult with an ART attorney in your home country to analyze any legal challenges. You also need to consult with an attorney in the destination country that is familiar with ART and immigration law to make sure that the procedures you are considering are legally permitted. For example, some countries abroad restrict medical care based on marital status or sexual orientation. Not only is it important to consult with an ART attorney, but it is vital to consult with an immigration attorney to ensure that the child will not have any issues returning to the home country and being deemed a legal citizen of the home country when born abroad via ART. The immigration attorneys also assist with obtaining the correct Consular Report of Abroad Birth, travel documents, and citizenship status for children born abroad.

With all of that said, foreign governments have been known to change the rules midstream and sometimes at the whim of a politician or his spouse (e.g., the president of the former Soviet Republic of Georgia pulled the plug on foreign adoption after his wife saw a report that upset her), the effect of which would be to strand your family in the foreign country, waiting for foreign and US authorities to figure out what the new rules mean and require. Trust us; it's not where you want to be with your newborn(s)!

Traveling with Frozen Genetic Material

Transporting frozen genetic material across the world is possible, but there are precautions to keep in mind when doing so. The chief challenge seen with the shipment of reproductive tissue outside of the United States into another country is finding a doctor or clinic that will accept the frozen genetic material and perform an embryo transfer. If certain ART procedures are illegal in the foreign country, the genetic material will not have a good home upon arrival if the procedures are not permitted. Furthermore, because each clinic uses different procedures to freeze and thaw reproductive tissue, the receiving laboratory may not be familiar

Your first trip with your kids abroad may in fact be the time you transport your frozen embryos from a clinic in the United States to an international clinic for an embryo transfer.

with the thawing and culturing procedures for the frozen genetic material and could potentially destroy it during the thawing process.

Have you ever arrived at the airport after a long flight to find that your duffle bag was destroyed and ripped open from travel wear and tear? Embryos are shipped in tanks filled with liquid nitrogen, and while the transportation of such embryos is usually fine, there is always the chance that something could happen to the tanks during transport or that customs agents in the foreign country demand that the tanks be open, thus destroying the precious cargo.

When genetic material is shipped from foreign counties into the United States, this subjects the reproductive tissue to the strict screening guidelines of the FDA. This may be problematic if the source of the genetic material was not initially tested according to FDA standards at an American FDA-licensed laboratory and cannot be retroactively tested in accordance with the guidelines because either the sperm or egg source is not available to be tested.

Learning Lessons with International ART from an ART Professional

Yifat Shaltiel, Esq., ART attorney and owner of Shaltiel Law Group, LLC and Surrogate Steps, LLC (www.surrogatesteps.com), shares important lessons learned from intended parents' experiences with international surrogacy:

> It is understandable why the United States has been a popular country for international intended parents. While the laws vary from state to state, most states laws are very favorable to surrogacy allowing international intended parents to have a surrogate in the United States, while still being recognized as the birth parents upon the birth of their child. Surrogacy has long been practiced in the United States, and prior to proceeding with a surrogate, the road to establishing parentage is clearly laid out. There are also many fertility clinics in the United States, most of whose pregnancy success rates are reported to the Society for Assisted Reproductive Technology. Furthermore, traveling with the child back to one's home country in most cases is a straightforward process since the child born via surrogacy in the United States is automatically a US citizen and is able to obtain a US passport. However, the benefits of the advanced medical technology and the evolution of the favorable surrogacy laws in the United States come at a price. The cost of surrogacy in the United States is approximately $100,000 and can be higher, whereas the costs of surrogacy in other countries are reported to be half of the costs of surrogacy in the United States.

> Many intended parents have successfully undergone the surrogacy process in countries outside the United States. Other intended parents, however, have not been as fortunate. For example, intended parent Rotem was a single parent who resided in Israel and sought to become a parent via gamete donation and surrogacy in Mexico. Despite the fact that surrogacy costs are reported to be lower in countries outside the United States, Rotem spent close to $100,000 and two years with no results

before deciding to proceed with surrogacy in the United States. Other parents Haseeb and Christy Amireh found themselves stuck in Mexico with their child born April 2015 due to the fact that the Mexican government has decided not to issue birth certificates to children born via surrogacy. Surrogate parents in Thailand have encountered similar issues, when in 2004 the Thai authorities decided to make compensated surrogacy illegal.

Understanding surrogacy laws in the country in which one chooses to pursue surrogacy is crucial. Intended parents Oren and Eldad knew the importance of proceeding with surrogacy in a country with favorable surrogacy laws. As a same-sex couple, Oren and Eldad were unable to pursue surrogacy in Israel, their home country. After considering that surrogacy laws have not yet evolved in Nepal and seeing the issues that many couples faced after Thailand outlawed compensated surrogacy, they decided to pursue surrogacy in the United States where the surrogacy laws are favorable. They knew that parentage would be established, creating no issues regarding travel back home, and that their child would have access to good medical care, especially in the case of a premature birth. Like many other international couples, Oren and Eldad felt that surrogacy in the United States would be safe.

Selecting a Fertility Clinic Abroad

While there are excellent fertility clinics abroad offering cutting-edge technology or less expensive services, there are certainly some bad eggs out there (once again, pun intended). It is important that a patient considering going abroad for fertility treatment do their homework when selecting a clinic. It is difficult to determine the expertise and quality of the physicians, embryologists, laboratory practices, and even clinic cleanliness when a clinic is far away and outside of your local community.

TIP

Check if the foreign clinic is part of a comparable organization to SART, in the foreign country that governs the quality of fertility clinics, or contact a local ministry of health in the clinic's home country for independent research.

The qualities you want to look for in fertility clinics abroad are similar to the qualities you want to look for in a domestic clinic, however it may be harder to obtain and understand the research on a foreign clinic. Factors to consider when researching a clinic abroad include reviewing success rates (verified by a national body or association), expertise and training of the medical professionals, costs, and quality and accreditations of the fertility clinic.

Fertility Tourism Concierge Service

Coordinating an international ART procedure is a full-time job for any intended parent when considering the long list of "to do" items to get from day one of the

process to bringing the baby home from the foreign country. Companies that specialize in international ART procedures and fertility tourism, called fertility tourism concierge services or fertility tourism agencies, guide intended parents as a case manager through each step of the international ART procedures to make the process flow easily. These companies provide focused attention to each detail on the international ART procedures taking place and facilitate medical needs, embryo shipment, matching with egg and/or surrogates abroad, travel arrangements, and coordinate legal arrangements with the applicable lawyers.

An example of the importance of carefully selecting your agency before proceeding and paying attention to red flags is seen with the highly publicized and devastating case of Planet Hospital. Planet Hospital, a former medical tourism business in California, expanded its services of international tummy tucks and hip replacements to include surrogacy in India, Thailand, and Mexico. Planet Hospital, with its heavy advertising and over 150 domain names, promised its customers cheap prices for international surrogacy, at around a 50 percent savings over surrogacy in the United States. They promised to deliver children, but instead delivered heartache to their victims, hopeful and eager intended parents. In the end, Planet Hospital was forced to file for bankruptcy and was investigated by the FBI as numerous furious clients who paid them between $20,000–$40,000 never saw results and never received a refund of a their money. Former clients of the agency shared red flag experiences of unpaid bills, reversed credit-card charges, and requests from Planet Hospital for more time and promises to "make it up" with free services. It was also reported that Planet Hospital engaged in unpermitted egg-splitting where eggs intended for one set of parents was split between multiple recipients.

> If it looks like a duck, swims like a duck, and quacks like a duck, then it probably is a duck. If a sketchy surrogacy or donor agency looks like a scam, acts like a scam, and sounds like a scam, think twice before paying them any money.

CAUTION

International Surrogacy and Egg Donation

According to Eloise Drane, CEO and founder of the surrogacy and egg donation agency Family Inceptions International (www.familyinceptions.com), "International surrogacy or egg donation is a surrogacy or egg donation arrangement in an overseas country. There are an increasing number of easily accessible overseas fertility treatments, depending on the service you need. Many of these clinics are high-quality clinics."

When dealing with ART procedures in any location, you must consider the laws in that jurisdiction as the laws and regulations vary greatly. As Drane points out regarding differences in procedures, "Many European countries, such as Spain, and South Africa do not show adult photos of the egg donors. In most countries all donors are anonymous. Furthermore, countries like South Africa and Greece limit the amount of compensation that a donor can receive per cycle.

In addition, you are not provided with many details of the donor's history unlike the United States. These are just some of the differences among countries.

"The media has focused on some of the negatives of international surrogacy in the potential for the exploitation of surrogates in third world countries. While bad practices do exist where surrogates are treated poorly," according to Drane who has experience arranging ART matters on an international scale, she believes that, "international treatment for egg donation or surrogacy can be a safe, cost effective way to have a child. Please, don't go blindly into reproductive tourism, or circumvent around to save money or time. However, anyone choosing this path must due their due diligence to ensure that they receive quality care and are not ripped off in the end. There are many reputable facilities in different countries. The question is which will be the best for you."

CHAPTER

7

Introduction to Egg, Sperm, and Embryo Donation

Gamete and embryo donation is the providing of egg, sperm, or embryos from one party to another in order to help an intended parent build a family. While the term *donation* is used, many times those that "donate" genetic material are compensated for the time, inconvenience, and discomfort associated with the screening and ovarian stimulation and egg retrieval (in the case of egg donors). For the donation of reproductive tissue, be it eggs, sperm, or embryos, the three main aspects to keep in mind that are addressed throughout this book include medical, legal, and psychological considerations.

There are levels of communication and disclosure between donors and recipients whereby donors are known, partially known, or anonymous donors. An intended parent can find a donor through an agency, frozen bank, fertility clinic, or self-matched (friends, family, or located on the Internet). The medical, legal, and psychological impacts on donation differ and need to be analyzed when dealing with a known, partially known, or anonymous donor and coupled with the method of locating your donor.

Known, Partially Known, and Anonymous Donors—Forms of Communication with a Donor

Do you want the ability to talk directly with your donor? Would you want to reach out to your donor directly or through a fertility clinic years down the road to research a possible genetic concern for the resulting child? This is a consideration that needs to be assessed with a mental health professional to analyze the short- and long-term risks and implications that differ among the forms of donation communication. The levels of communication between donor and recipient are not black and white. There is a sliding scale ranging from a completely anonymous donation, with no future communication with the donor, all the way up to the recipient becoming best friends with the donor and everything in between.

Known Donor

Known donation does not necessarily mean that the donor is your "bestie" once the donation is complete. While many known donors are friends or family offering to donate genetic material to help build a family, a known donor is one with whom the intended parents have open communication with the source of the genetic donated material. The parties know each other's names, contact information, and have the ability within their legal documentation (hopefully if they have the proper documents in place) to remain in communication.

An open donation is considered important to some intended parents. Open donation allows for the ongoing development of a future relationship with the donor. This can be beneficial for an emotional reason and also for medical purposes, as it allows the parties to remain in communication in the event a genetic issue should arise in the future with the child or the donor. With any form of donation, it is imperative that the proper legal documentation is in place to make certain that the donor relinquishes any and all parental rights and that the intended parents assume any and all parental rights to the resulting child. It is essential to document this form of open communication in the parties' contract. In this type of arrangement, the parties' legal names are likely to be included on the donation contract.

Partially Known

While there are variations of partially known donations, generally this is an arrangement wherein the information shared between the intended parents and the donor is somewhat limited. As an example, the parties may decide they want to meet in person, but they do not want to exchange contact information or continue an open relationship. Thereafter, following the donation all future communication is performed through the clinic, agency, or donation bank. Assuming that the proper legal documentation is in place for the donation, the form of future communication between the intended parents and donor will be established in writing. In this type of arrangement, the parties' legal names may be included on the donation contract or the parties may choose to sign the contract anonymously by an identification number assigned to the donor.

Anonymous

Anonymous donation is a closed form of donation where the intended parents do not communicate directly with the donor and do not have the donor's name, but instead, identify the donor with an anonymous ID number. Any necessary communication between intended parents and the donor is channeled through the clinic, agency, or donor bank that serves as a middle man and provides any information needed regarding the genetic materials donated. An anonymous donation arrangement does not guarantee that the parties will forever remain anonymous to one another. Even though the parties do not share identifying information, with the power of the Internet and the ability to locate a person just based on a photo, there is always a chance that donors and intended parents can be located.

In this type of donation, the donor is requested to update and keep current the clinic, agency, or donor bank of the discovery of future health matters that may impact the child. However, people move on with their lives, and there can be no guarantee that the donor will forever be interested in providing such updates and information.

Assuming the proper legal documentation is in place for the donation, the anonymous communication between the intended parents and donor is established in writing whereby the parties may agree to be contacted in the future for medical necessity but only through an intermediary such as the clinic, agency, or donor bank. In this type of arrangement, the parties' legal names are not included on the donation contract and the parties sign the contract anonymously by donor ID number.

The Donor Sibling Registry (DSR)

When a person donates egg, sperm, or embryos, assuming the proper legal guidelines are followed, they relinquish all parental rights to the resulting child. What happens if in the future, the donor conceived person or donor wants to connect, either for the purpose of obtaining critical genetic information or just out of curiosity as to what the other person is up to in this world. A further consideration is what if a donor, years after donating their genetic material, discovers they have a serious genetic family history and are unable to contact the intended parents or donor conceived person through the clinic or agency?

For people born as a result of donated egg, sperm, or embryos, there is an online and voluntary registry available, with a database spanning the world, to locate genetic relatives if both people want to be located. The Donor Sibling Registry (DSR) is a website and nonprofit organization in the United States that provides a community to allow donor-conceived people the opportunity to locate medical and health information from their biological donors, allow donors to share family, ancestral, and genetic details with offspring, and allow for half-siblings to connect, among other resources relating to donation. When visiting the DSR, those looking to find a biological donor or half-sibling can search the database by the donor's birthday, donor type, donor ID number, or facility the donation occurred.

Introduction to Egg Donation

It is evident that the process of egg donation is quite different than the process of sperm donation. Sperm donation simply requires a man's "special time" in a room with a racy magazine and usually no physician involvement, while the medical process of egg donation is significantly more cumbersome and potentially problematic.

Sperm banks have existed in the United States since the 1950, yet the popularity of egg donation has only grown over the past ten years. Since the egg donation process is relatively new in the overall history of assisted reproduction, processes and regulations as to this practice are still forming just as technology and legal issues continue to evolve.

According to SART, there are four main medical reasons why people need to use an egg donor: (1) ovarian failure, (2) women who carry a serious genetic disease and who wish to minimize the chance that the disease will be passed on to their children; (3) women whose age is sufficiently advanced so that their fertility potential is impaired significantly; and, (4) women who have had poor-quality embryos during previous IVF cycles.[6] In addition to the medical needs requiring an egg donor, the biggest practical need seen in the ART world is that of male same-sex couples or a single man since science has not progressed far enough to eliminate the need of an egg for this population.

Each month a woman should produce one egg. However, with the egg donation process, coupled with the assistance of ART, egg donors' ovaries are stimulated with hormone medications, while under the medical care of the reproductive physician, to help create numerous eggs for retrieval and ultimate donation. Keep in mind when reading each section relating to egg donation that an intended parent is not just receiving just one egg from the donor but are instead hopefully receiving numerous eggs to use for ART. Being an egg donor is like going through half of IVF. They undergo the ovary stimulation and egg retrieval components but do not complete the second half of IVF, which is the embryo transfer into the uterus.

A fertility clinic that is performing an egg retrieval must not allow the egg donor to begin her fertility medications until the proper egg donor contract is fully executed between the egg donor (her partner or spouse) and intended parents. Some fertility clinics have their own egg donation contracts; nonetheless, a proper legal contract needs to be fully executed by all parties before the real medical procedures begin. This protects all parties involved.

As it relates to egg donation, aspects of the process to consider are the cost for an egg donor, the compensation to an egg donor, the medication implications for the egg donor, and privacy between the donor and recipient.

According to Chicago-based egg donor and surrogacy agency ConceiveAbilities (http://www.conceiveabilities.com), "along with compensation, the intended parents pay the costs of the screening and all medical aspects, including the premium and any deductible for the supplemental short-term accidental health insurance policy. Donors also receive a 1099 tax form at the end of the year for compensation earned. The only cost to the donor is a current [P]ap smear and local transportation. Egg donor compensation covers the time, effort, inconvenience and high level of commitment necessary to accomplish the process. Our program places expectations on the donor to follow through. Compensation should mirror the importance placed on her commitment and generosity."

In qualifying a woman to act as an egg donor, ConceiveAbilities shares that "professionals involved in the screening process look very carefully at motivation, health and family medical history, and emotional stability (among other factors). All of these things are weighed, and often it is no one thing that disqualifies a donor candidate. However, missing scheduled appointments without informing

---

[6]http://www.sart.org/detail.aspx?id=1894

the professionals involved is typically the leading cause of disqualification. Due to the time-sensitive nature of the procedures, the ability to keep a schedule is one of the most important aspects of the process." While there is a fairly standard protocol for creating eggs for a donor, the medical treatment will be determined by the fertility doctor and is customized for each donor.

Where to Obtain an Egg Donor

For whatever reason a person needs an egg donor, and regardless of whether the intended parents want an anonymous or known donor, there are a variety of options on how to locate an egg donor. The main resources to locate an egg donor are through an egg donor agency, a frozen egg bank, a fertility clinic, or self-matched through friends, family, or the Internet. Each method for locating an egg donor has different processes involved.

Egg Donor Agency or Egg Donation Matching Entities

According to Florida-based egg donor and surrogacy agency, Open Arms Consultants (http://www.openarmsconsultants.com), "the agency's role in your egg donation journey is to provide you with a suitable candidate that has met the ASRM (American Society of Reproductive Medicine) expectations of a quality egg donor. Although there are not legal requirements, most reputable agencies and clinics will operate within the guidelines set forth by the ASRM. Some agencies are partnered with a fertility clinic and the egg donors offered may have had preliminary medical screening, but other agencies do not have the medical affiliation. In those cases, unless the egg donor is experienced, there will most likely be no genetic testing or screenings completed."

The egg donor agency not only locates an egg donor for intended parents but it facilitates the egg donor in attending the various appointments for her psychological and medical screening and helps coordinate the logistics of the entire egg donation process, thus making it easier for the intended parents. Practices for egg donor agencies differ throughout the country and the world, and there is not one model for an egg donation program, but typically, several steps are in place when using an agency to locate an egg donor.

The egg donor agency locates and interviews the prospective egg donor to learn preliminary information on the donor such as her interests, lifestyle, background, and general health. The agency has the capacity to perform some preliminary screenings on the donor such as a criminal background check, intelligence quotient (IQ) test, personality test, and possibly some limited medical tests, thus initially weaning out poor candidates. A good egg donor agency has very stringent criteria when selecting an egg donor and are selective as to the women they allow into the program.

Want a blue-eyed, blond-haired baby? Go for it! When selecting an egg donor with an agency, many times through the agency's online database, the intended parents can enter certain criteria they are looking for in a donor (physical characteristics, education, ethnicity, and/or religious affiliation) and are provided with corresponding extensive profiles of the donors. This usually includes background on the donor, a personal biography, education information, health and reproductive history, family and genetic history, and possibly childhood and adult photographs. Some egg donation agencies provide audio and/or video tapes of the donors.

Some additional helpful tips for the egg donation process shared by Open Arms Consultants include:

- Get a copy of your egg donor's profile from your agency. You may need to reference back to her if you want to do another egg retrieval for a sibling cycle.
- Don't be afraid to ask questions about your egg donor if you want to know more about her. The egg donor will share as much as she's comfortable and the agency will work as the buffer between the two of you.
- Many egg donors are excited to help a family. Write a letter to your egg donor expressing your gratitude if you are inclined to.
- Remember that the egg donation cycle is time sensitive. There are many factors involved when an agency is coordinating a cycle. Be sure to understand their communication style and request regular updates. Keep in mind that nothing may be happening as sometimes it's just about waiting for an appointment to happen or waiting on other parties to respond. Do your part timely to reduce the chance of having to start the cycle all over again.
- Be patient and determined with the process. Sometimes there are obstacles that will cause delays, but work with your agency to get through them.

How to Pick an Egg Donor Agency

When hiring an egg donation agency, it is important to research the company and also carefully review the company's retainer contract. Some intended parents hire an attorney to review the agency contract to make sure they are protected.

According to Open Arms Consultants, "when you have made your final choice for your egg donor, you will have to officially hire your agency. This may be done with signing a retainer or agreement that will distinguish the responsibilities of the agency and outline the "what ifs." Be sure to read thoroughly what the agency will do in the event that your egg donor is medically disqualified or if your egg donor does not comply with the medical instructions or other cycle expectations. Also review how the situation will be handled if your egg donor withdraws before and after you have incurred expenses related to her. How many times will the agency rematch you with a different donor and what will be the circumstances? What is their refund policy?"

Another very important aspect of hiring an egg donor agency according to Open Arms Consulting is "how they will or will not manage the escrow account/egg donor expenses. How are they making decisions with your money and how involved are you expected to be? If the donor cycle is not a "known" cycle, the agency will have to work to maintain anonymity between you, your money, and your egg donor. You should be provided with an estimation of costs prior to hiring the agency and then an accounting report with how your funds are used. Your agency should be very transparent with the financial expectations when you have chosen your egg donor. If she is experienced, she may already have some things completed that you should not have to pay for again such as a psychological evaluation (if it's within the last twelve months) or genetic testing results if she has donated before. Her increased compensation will offset these saved costs. Most agencies will not manage your financial responsibility to the fertility clinic so it will be your responsibility to make sure you are taking care of all of your obligations to prevent any unnecessary delays with your cycle."

Similar to surrogacy agencies, egg donation agencies are not regulated or licensed by a governmental agency like physicians or attorneys. Former ART patient and current ART advocate, Marisa Horowitz-Jaffe, shares her experience of hiring an illegitimate egg donor agency:

CAUTION

The lack of regulation over egg donor agencies can lead to potentially fraudulent activity or simply the agency can cause more problems for the already stressed out intended parents.

By the summer of 2009, my husband and I had experienced such imaginable tragedy that we could hardly think straight. Well, at least that's what I like to tell myself years later as a form of mentally compensating for how we were able to get scammed by an egg donor and surrogacy "agency." At the age of thirty, we decided to start building our family and nothing was working, and we were eventually classified as "unexplained infertility." IVFs #1 through #6 ended in either miscarriage or negatives. We gave donor eggs a shot on IVF #7 using the in-house donor pool at our very large New York City clinic. It worked the first cycle, and we were overjoyed. Tragically, at twenty weeks, the baby quietly passed away in my womb, and all his testing came back as a healthy fetus. Again, it was chalked up to "unexplained."

It took a few months for us to get back on track and start investigating surrogacy and yet another egg donor. We had already been working with a very small and wonderful surrogacy agency who matched us with a wonderful surrogate in Dallas, Texas. We flew down to accompany her and her husband for the initial physical exam at the local IVF clinic we were going to use. The staff was warm and nurturing, and one of the nurses mentioned that they just had a great egg donor come in a few months ago, and she was looking to donate again soon. The only issue was, "the agency this woman goes through is not one we like to work with here; we have had numerous issues with them. However, this specific donor is responsible, mature, and wonderful. If you like, here's the number for the agency."

Oh, if only I had heeded the warning of that nurse! But we were so distraught; I had no more mental space to do one more iota of research and calling and investigating. I blindly and happily clutched that scrap of paper with what I just knew would be the way to my magic donor. I called the next day, spoke to a very well-spoken woman (who turned out to be the owner and sole employee) who empathized with our tragedies and assured us that yes, that donor is ready and willing to donate again . . . just as soon as we express over $5,000 for the agency fee. The money was sent within twenty-four hours, even though I did feel it was a little odd to spend so much money on an agency that didn't do any searching or work for us. I also took a look at some donor profiles she had sent me, and they all almost looked to have been cut out and pasted by a child, with photographs and written information haphazardly written on sheets that were poorly scanned and emailed to me. More red flags that I swallowed down.

I wish I had done a simple Google search. I would have found numerous horrible reviews of her, read how her surrogates are rarely paid on time, her egg donors are still waiting for compensation, and intended parents are often left hanging. We were one of those left hanging. Within weeks of securing our donor (so we thought), we began receiving cryptic emails from the woman at the "agency" that the donor had been in a slight car accident, the ER doctor told her to immediately stop her IVF suppression meds, and all of this other gibberish. But we kept on plugging because we had to, the alternative was not feasible. After months of being led along on a string, we got the law involved to demand our money back, yet we only received about half of it because we had signed a legal contract with her. Six months later the "agency" closed, leaving numerous surrogates, IPs, and donors out in the cold. She was eventually called out on it, and she filed for bankruptcy. We were never given an apology or the rest of our money back.

This woman took full advantage of our tragedies and extremely fragile mental state. She knew we would spend any amount of money to make this pain go away. After speaking to other victims, we learned she used a similar story and tactic again and again. Final thought—do your research. Investigate, speak to former clients. Never hand over money if you have a nagging feeling in your gut.

Frozen Egg Banks

Sperm and embryos have been successfully frozen and utilized for decades. With the advancements in technology for freezing reproductive tissue called *vitrification* (the solidification of a solution without ice crystallization), as of 2012, the freezing of eggs for use in procreation is no longer considered experimental and the concept of egg freezing is now in common ART parlance. In fact, the notion of egg freezing is so popular that major tech companies, such as Apple and Facebook, are offering cash incentives and paying up to $20,000 for female employees to freeze their eggs as part of the companies' health insurance plans. Do we see Apple coming out with an iEgg in the future?

Women are born with all of the eggs they will ever have in a lifetime, which is about 1–2 million eggs. By the time a woman reaches puberty, she is left with about half a million eggs, and as much as women hate to think about this, the egg reserve continues to decrease as they age, especially as women enter their mid- to late 30s and 40s. Not only does the egg quantity diminish, but the quality of eggs is negatively impacted—hence the increasing popularity of egg freezing. Research indicates that success rates for using frozen donor egg is rapidly approaching and is nearly the same as using fresh donor eggs.

In using a frozen egg bank, intended parents can choose from a database of screened and psychologically analyzed egg donors for use in an IVF procedure. They can base their choice on a variety of characteristics such as physical appearance, face, religion, education, blood type, etc. The intended parents may also review medical and personal history, donor essays, audio interviews, and childhood photos, depending on the company's resources and policy.

Fertility Clinics

More often now fertility clinics are becoming a one-stop shop for ART patients for they can have their own pools of egg donors to choose from. These are typically anonymous and can include fresh and/or frozen egg donors. The procedures for obtaining a donor egg from a fertility clinic is similar to that of an egg donor agency or frozen egg bank, but the prices and administrative procedures will differ depending on the clinic.

Self-Matched

You may have a friend or family member that has graciously offered to donate their eggs to you. With the increasing popularity of social media forums and online resources, some people can locate an egg donor over the Internet. When considering this path of self-matching, especially when you know the donor, it is imperative that you consider the psychological implications to determine whether all parties are able to handle the future relationship between the child, donor, and intended parents. Broken record repeated warning (or broken Ipod, for the younger generation), parties must have the proper legal documentation in place for self-matched donation, even if the donor verbally promises to waive parental rights or if such promises are made by a handshake—that will not protect you!

Picking a Good Egg

While at the grocery store, you pick up a carton of eggs, check if they are cracked, and take the best carton of eggs you can find. Although the human egg cell (ovum or oocyte) is the largest human cell in the body, measuring 0.15 to 0.2 mm and is just visible to the naked eye, picking an egg for ART is based on numerous considerations, not just how the egg looks in the carton.

Egg donor and surrogacy agency ConceiveAbilitites shares their professional expertise on the top ten signs of a good egg donor:

1. You have a giving spirit. As a top egg donor agency, we seek women who are intent on creating a win-win situation. By donating eggs to intended parents, you give them the opportunity to make their dreams come true. In turn, we hope to help you as well through compensation for your time and effort.
2. You're healthy: physically and mentally. Egg donors must have a generally healthy personal and family medical history.
3. You're between [the] ages 21–29. While some agencies will accept an 18-year-old donor, we require donors to be at least 21. This is to protect her reproductive health and ensure she is old enough to understand the risks and emotional magnitude of donating eggs.
4. You're a tough cookie and not afraid of a few little needles. Yes, needles—in the form of blood draws and self-injected medication—are requirements of egg donation. But most women find it to be far less intimidating than they expected, and some really enjoy the responsibility of it all!

5. Your schedule has some flexibility. We understand that you work, attend school, or have other strict schedules to keep, so [we'll] do our best to accommodate you. Scheduling conflicts occur, though, and egg donors should expect to be flexible and patient.

6. You don't smoke. Egg donors must be 100% nicotine and drug-free for the duration of their participation in our egg donor program.

7. You need money to pay for school or for travel. Compensation is certainly a perk of the process! You are compensated for your time and inconvenience, but that short period is rewarded with the opportunity to make your own dreams come true.

8. When you start something you finish it. Being part of an egg donation program isn't something that can be taken lightly. Once you've committed to the process, you have an entire team of people—including hopeful intended parents—counting on your ability to follow through.

9. You're Asian, East Indian, or Jewish. While we accept egg donors of all ethnic backgrounds, the fact is that Asian, East Indian, and Jewish women are always in high demand and often receive higher compensation for this reason.

10. Making others happy makes you happy! There's not much more of a reward in this world than helping make someone's dream come true. And the dream of a family is a powerful one! If the idea of helping to create a family makes you giddy, we'd love to welcome you to our program.

Egg Sharing

Some egg donation programs offer the concept of egg sharing, where one donor's eggs are shared between multiple intended parents, which helps reduce the cost of the donation, but also increases the problem of possible half-siblings being born to different intended parents.

As a potential medical consideration with egg sharing for the donor, if a donor has to undergo multiple egg stimulation and retrieval processes to have a successful IVF for the various intended parents, this could negatively impact the donor's future egg supply and her ability to build her own family. Psychological impacts on the donor should be analyzed as to whether she can mentally accept that she may have biological children with multiple families and that she has no legal rights to those children. Some frown upon the concept of egg sharing as the commodification of human life and equate it to an indirect form of buying a child.

Introduction to Sperm Donation

The use of donated sperm for human conception can be traced back to the eighteenth century, yet the ability to successfully freeze, store, and thaw sperm for procreation was not established until the early twentieth century. In recent ART history, the use of donor sperm has decreased as the use of intracytoplasmic sperm injection (ICSI) for the treatment of male infertility has become utilized more often at fertility clinics. Coupled with the emergence of acquired immunodeficiency syndrome (AIDS), sperm donation within the fertility clinic context is performed exclusively with sperm that has been frozen and quarantined to test for sexually transmitted diseases.

There are two main reasons why a man will choose to have his sperm frozen: (1) to preserve his fertility in a situation where he may be undergoing a medical treatment such as radiation or surgery that may render him infertile and to use the sperm for his own purposes, or (2) to make an extra hundred bucks and help another person who needs donated sperm to build a family.

When sperm is donated for reproductive purposes, it can be inseminated directly into the intended mother or surrogate through the process of artificial insemination (this source of sperm can be fresh or frozen), or it can be combined with a retrieved egg from the intended mother or egg donor and then transferred into the intended mother or surrogate through the process of IVF (this is accomplished exclusively through the use of frozen sperm).

As many women say, "It's so much harder being a woman than a man!" In the ART context when it comes to donating genetic material, that is very true. You have to giggle when you think about the difference in how eggs are surgically retrieved from a woman, involving hormones, injections, and even anesthesia, compared to the method by which the seed of life is obtained from a man.

In the general method, a donor provides his ejaculate through masturbation. Other methods of retrieval include an electrical stimulator or a special condom, known as a *collection condom*, used to collect the semen during intercourse. Unless the sperm is directly inseminated in an intended mother/surrogate by intercourse (not recommended, it is a huge medical and legal risk!), or inseminated fresh by an at-home insemination kit (also proceed with medical and legal caution!), the sperm is frozen and quarantined, usually for a period of six months or in accordance with current FDA and applicable safety guidelines, and the donor is retested prior to the sperm being used for procreation.

A large segment of litigation in the ART world arises as a result of sperm being donated without the proper legal precautions. These cases typically stem from undocumented sperm donation arrangements, which can threaten the parental rights and create unintended obligations of all parties involved. It is imperative that before intended parents receive donated sperm, that the sperm donor, his spouse or partner, and the intended parents sign the proper legal documents. In addition to the medical and legal considerations with donated sperm, the use of donated sperm (either with known or anonymous donors) implicates psychological considerations that should be assessed with a mental health professional, not only for the sperm donor but for the intended parents as well. Such psychological considerations include how to inform the future child and family members of the parties involved about the use of a sperm donor, the possibility that different intended parents may share a sperm donor and have half-siblings with different legal parents, and the type of communication the sperm donor and intended parents intend to have in the future, if any.

Where to Obtain Donated Sperm

The most common places intended parents procure donated sperm are as follows:

Sperm Banks

Sperm banks, also known as *cryobanks*, collect and store sperm and offer andrology laboratory services such as semen analysis, frozen donor sperm services, and long-term storage for sperm specimens.

The intended parents obtaining sperm from a sperm bank typically review an anonymous database of eligible sperm donors identified by donor numbers and can search the database based on the donor's physical characteristics, race, ethnicity, educational background, and other criteria. Sperm banks vary in the background information they provide on donors and some provide childhood and adult pictures, videos, or audio tapes, handwriting samples, and IQ tests. For additional fees, some sperm banks promise a certain sperm donor is an "exclusive donor," whose sperm is only used for one intended recipient. Note however that this promise is impossible to regulate or enforce.

Fertility Clinics

Some fertility clinics allow for the collection of donated sperm and either match the intended parents with a donor (similar to the method of a sperm bank), or the clinic facilitates a known donor to deposit his sperm at the clinic's facilities for testing, sperm analysis, freezing, and subsequent use for the intended parents, all subject to the strict FDA guidelines and screening methods of the particular clinic, which includes genetic testing and other semen analysis processes.

Private or Directed Donation

Intended parents may have a friend, family member, or may locate someone from the Internet directly to act as their sperm donor. There are also sperm donor brokers and various websites that assist intended parents in finding a sperm donor for use in conception. Generally these types of sperm donation relationships are "known donations" (especially with family and friend donors), but can also be arranged as a "partially known" or anonymous donation if the parties are introduced through a broker. Private donations that do not go through the proper channels of testing that is performed with sperm banks or fertility clinics may be less expensive, but at a much greater cost relating to safety and legal liability.

When sperm is obtained by a private or directed donation, the sperm source can be properly screened by the fertility clinic and safely used for conception. However, when the sperm source is inseminated either through an at-home insemination kit or through direct insemination by the donor (i.e., sex between the sperm donor and intended mother/surrogate), this raises medical and legal risks for the parties involved.

A Woman's Journey with Sperm Donation

Alice Crisci, cancer survivor, infertility advocate, and founder of the nonprofit organization helping women with cancer to access fertility treatment called Fertile Action, shares her experience in using donor sperm in her fertility journey:

Early on in my breast cancer diagnosis, I learned cancer treatments can cause infertility. Chemotherapy can throw a young woman into a permanent state of menopause, subsequently causing infertility. Tamoxifen, an oral tablet usually prescribed for five years for those with an estrogen-sensitive cancer (meaning estrogen causes your cancer to grow) is known to harm the fetus. Doctors and the National Cancer Institute advise against pregnancy while taking the drug.

Yet again, cancer forced me to look at my future and ask: Am I willing to take the gamble that I will be fertile when I conclude all my cancer treatments at age 37? For some women who regain fertility it can take six months to two years. By then, I will be 39. Is that when I want to start having children at 39? Or will I invest in my future as a biological mom by choosing a sperm donor literally from a catalog and freezing eggs or embryos? The latter option was the last thing I thought I would ever be thinking about this year or any year. With resoluteness, I chose to not let cancer eliminate any possibilities for my future, including that dream I had of being a mom before the age of 39, even if it meant using a surrogate for my frozen embryos.

I scheduled a phone consult with Dr. Wendy Chang of the Southern California Reproductive Center (SCRC). Serendipitously, when I spoke to Dr. Chang I was on day two of my period. After she explained my risk factors and the process, she informed me I would have to start my hormone injections to stimulate the follicles on my ovaries the next day or not at all given the tight timeframe before my double-mastectomy. At 5 p.m. on a Tuesday, I made yet another monumental decision catalyzed by cancer and called my dear friend Jen for my first of many rides to the fertility clinic.

We arrived for my 7 a.m. ultrasound and blood work. By 10 a.m. I was in the business manager's office with Jen learning of the enormous costs associated with fertility preservation. While Jen discussed whether there was financial aid available for cancer patients, I was on the phone with my American Express card asking for a rather large limit increase. We walked out of the clinic with my first round of hormone injections as well as the significant financial investment in my future as a mommy charged to my AMEX, earning me what I've dubbed "fertility miles."

It took me about a week of hormone injections to decide if I wanted to freeze eggs or embryos. Embryos have a much higher likelihood of producing a child later in life than frozen eggs alone. I was hoping for a ½ and ½ scenario so one day if I do get married, my husband and I can try my eggs first, and if I'm lucky, one might fertilize.

Dr. Chang's staff gave me a package of information for the California Cryobank, an apparently renowned sperm bank. It felt so unnatural and weird, especially the first time you look at the catalog. I had to narrow down my first choices from hundreds of donors, which as I was told "change frequently due to supply and demand." I was so overwhelmed at first, but comforted by the fact the sperm bank only accepted 1 percent of all applicants. They did more screenings on these donors than a government employee gets when vying for a top secret security clearance.

I first narrowed down donor potentials from a catalog that gave only the basic stats on the donors: height, weight, nationality, basic features, profession, and whether or not it was known if the donors' sperm had produced a child for someone already. (Yes, there is a sibling registry, thank God, so my child one day will hopefully not accidentally marry their sibling.) There are also six different pieces of data that a donor may have provided: a baby picture, audio interview, personality test, a written essay, and staff impressions. Every donor is required to fill out a very extensive profile that includes the medical history of extended family on both their mother's and father's side of the family.

I started my search with darker skinned donors of ethnic backgrounds that I was naturally attracted to and ruled out those who did not complete all six possible pieces of information. I miraculously narrowed it down to six potential donors. The sperm bank then conducted what is called a photo-matching service where I supplied a photo and they sync up your features with the donors; I guess to make sure you aesthetically could create a decent looking child together. They scored each one on attractiveness and how close of a match we were. My six prospects were between 8.5 matching and 7.0. Most people don't ever score higher than an 8.5 so I began purchasing some of the available reports in order of my preference (yes, every additional report that is not in the catalog is provided for a fee). Cancer costs at this point are out of control.

I first used their written essays to narrow the choices down further. I thought if I could somehow hear their voice in the written word, looking at their handwriting, I may find something intuitively that worked for me. After connecting with two out of the six essays, I then ordered their full package: a $70 investment per donor.

It was between a tall Italian or a shorter Spanish, French, Mexican. I didn't know it was possible to fall in love with DNA, but I did. I am in love with the short Spanish, French, Mexican medical student with tall uncles on both sides of the family. Since he was only 5'8" himself, I wanted to make sure there was a chance for some height, given I am only 5'3". He seemed very smart (high SAT scores!) with the most spotless medical history of any donor I read about. His essay revealed similar values to mine, and his responses so fully matched my take on life. In fact, they made me want to meet him, though I knew it wasn't possible.

Turns out he was a competitive baseball player (I was the first girl to play baseball in an all-boys league when I was twelve), and his younger sister was a dancer (I switched from sports to performance dance in college). When choosing someone's DNA, it became very important to me that athleticism and rhythm ran in the family!

In the end, I literally was so in love with my sperm choice that I wanted to have a baby right away. Of course, that sentiment may have been hormonally induced because there were thirty-one eggs growing inside of me. My sister said, "You have one egg for every year you've been alive!" Sometimes, she notices the funniest things.

Up until my scheduled egg retrieval, I loved the process my body was going through. I administered the hormone injections into my belly day and night. The increased hormonal stimulation at first made me very happy, sensual, and more womanly than I had ever felt before. I've always had a lean physique and before cancer had some typical body image issues. I thought I would hate the "fat" part of getting pregnant. But as my belly expanded from my ovaries growing and the constipation they neglected to tell me about in advance, I could stand sideways and kind of look pregnant. For the first time, I declared, "I'm going to be so cute pregnant!" (Yeah, clearly the body image issues disappear with cancer.)

I could literally feel life force growing inside my body, and it brought me great comfort, joy, and hope for my future. I could see light coming back to my eyes, the dark cancer window shade lifting up long enough for me to visualize a little girl with long, dark curly hair dancing in the middle of the family room with me, her mommy.

Introduction to Embryo Donation

During the IVF process, it is common that people have extra viable embryos available to be frozen. Frozen embryos cannot be kept at home in a freezer but instead are shipped to long-term storage facilities to "chill." Embryos can be frozen for an indefinite amount of time. which can lead to great expense for the intended parents to pay for the storage facilities that hold the frozen embryos. If the family who created these embryos decides that the embryos are no longer needed for their family planning—hopefully because there was success in the process prior to utilization of all of the embryos—that family can choose to donate the "extra" embryos to others.

The ultimate success with donated embryos depends on the quality of the embryos at the time that they were frozen, the age of the woman who provided the eggs for the donated embryo, and the number of embryos transferred into the recipient. While the recipients of a donated embryo will not have a genetic link to the resulting child, it will allow them to experience pregnancy and birth, and control the course of the pregnancy that may not be possible in an adoption.

Amy Demma, Esq. (http://www.lawofficesofamydemma.com) is a New York attorney and ART advocate providing services to those engaged in assisted family building, specifically egg, embryo, and known-sperm donation as well as surrogacy. Amy shares her expertise on the various steps involved in the embryo-donation process:

1. **Clinic Clearance:** The first step is to determine at which clinic the prospective recipients will be able to do the frozen embryo transfer. I recommend that the recipients call their clinic to inquire as to whether or not they offer donor embryos services and, further, will that clinic accept cryo'd embryos created at another facility? If applicable, recipients also need to determine if that clinic will accept donation of cryo'd embryos created with donor egg. Before any next steps, we first have to identify a clinic for the cycle. On several embryo donation cases, I have assisted the parties in "clinic shopping" as not all IVF clinics work with donated embryos.
2. **Medical Clearance:** Is the recipient mom (or gestational carrier) cleared for frozen embryo transfer with donated embryos? If recipient mom is of advanced age (usually over the age of forty-five), she likely will have to seek clearance from her primary care physician and/or other medical

clearance that might include an EKG, a stress test, a mammogram, or whatever else the clinic deems necessary in order for the recipient mom to be considered appropriate for a donor embryo cycle. If recipient mom is younger than forty-five and otherwise healthy, she may be presumed medically cleared. Still, both donors and recipients should confirm that the clinic intended to perform the embryo donation will accept the recipient mom as their patient. Depending on how current the recipient mom's medical records are, getting medical clearance could take months.

3. **Embryological Clearance:** Has the clinic intended to perform the embryo donation reviewed the embryology report of the embryos being considered and do the embryos meet that clinic's criteria for donation? Every clinic has their own criteria for clearing embryos for embryo donation. If there is a cost related to getting records from donor's clinic to recipients, cost is usually picked up by the prospective recipients.

4. **Psychological Clearance:** I don't advise that the parties proceed to psych clearance until clinic, medical and embryological clearance is in place, especially if the parties are known or to become known. Essentially we first answer: is the donation feasible, before we have the parties (separately, if anonymous, or perhaps together, if known—depends on clinic policy) meet with a mental health professional. If after independent psych clearance is issued (yes, the recipients pay for the donors' visit) then or if parties are known or intending to become known, the clinic may request a joint psych visit. Again, policies at each clinic vary regarding the process by which parties considering embryo donation (both donor and recipients) are psych cleared so the recipients should inquire with the clinic as to what will be required for that clearance. All costs related to obtaining psychological clearance are borne by the recipients; however, in my experience, if the donors are not local to the recipients' clinic, they likely will be able to meet with a local mental health professional and can avoid travel.

5. **Legal Clearance:** While the above clearances are being attended to, the attorney representing the embryo donors should inquire as to whether or not the embryo donation involves embryos created with donor egg. If this is the case, the egg donation contract (if there was one) will be reviewed to determine if the egg donor must first issue her consent for the embryo donation. Some IVF clinics as well as storage facilities may also require (regardless of what the egg donation contract reads) that the egg donor be notified and issue consent for the embryo donation. Reaching the egg donor and obtaining her consent may take some time; be prepared for this and allow for a delay in the embryo donation, as this and all other clearances are pending. Once we have all the clearances in place, the recipients' attorney will begin to draft the embryo donation contract. The recipients pay for both the donors' attorney as well as their own legal counsel. The attorney that drafted the embryo donation will issue to the IVF clinic a letter of legal clearance, and the donors can then proceed with having the embryos transported to the IVF clinic.

CHAPTER

8

ART Resources

Infertility is a syndrome that has huge implications on those suffering from it. Books offer guidance and understanding about how to cope with challenges raised by ART. Jump on the Internet and there are numerous infertility messages boards, social media support groups, and the like of every variety. Whatever subgroup you fit in, be it same-sex couple, heterosexual single, gay single, Italian gay amputee single, there's a group of like-minded friends that can make you feel less alone during what can be an isolating experience.

Beyond Internet groups, there are organizations that provide education, empowerment, support groups, and guidance for those struggling within the world of ART and infertility. Some organizations are wide-ranging, with no affiliation to a particular religion or sexual orientation. Other groups are geared toward more specific backgrounds and some find this more comforting and easier to relate to while going through a similar experience. Below are just a few examples of the incredible organizations offering support and other services for those going through ART.

Uprooted

People suffering from infertility come in all shapes and sizes. They have different economic, cultural, ethnic, and religious backgrounds. In many religious communities, it can be isolating to those that suffer from infertility when this topic is taboo. While infertility often evokes negative feelings, it can also result in beautiful responses from those that have gone through this experience and thus making it easier for others.

Uprooted cofounder, Dalia Davis shared that "[i]nfertility isolates, the Jewish community should not," which lead her and co-founder Becca Shimshak to create Uprooted. Both women were touched by some form of infertility and saw the need for an organization to support other Jewish people going through this difficult process and created the organization Uprooted, a Jewish response to infertility (http://www.weareuprooted.org/). When summarizing Uprooted, Davis emphasizes that "[o]ur goal is to be there for people before, during, and after their fertility journeys. Additionally we see Uprooted as a pluralistic organization—pluralistic in that we seek to be relevant and helpful for Jews from all walks of Judaism—our team represents a spectrum of different approaches to Judaism. We are also pluralistic in how we approach fertility journeys—we seek to be relevant and helpful to Jews who are trying to build their family in any and every way they chose to do so. We have no agenda in terms of how people go about this journey we simply hope to support them throughout the process. We are blessed to have a number of different fertility experiences among our team as well."

Resolve

RESOLVE, the National Infertility Association (http://www.resolve.org), is a nonprofit organization with the only established, nationwide network mandated to promote reproductive health and to ensure equal access to all family-building options for men and women experiencing infertility or other reproductive disorders. Across the country, RESOLVE offers free peer lead infertility support groups that offer incredible support to those in need and empowers people with the education needed to better traverse the minefield of the ART world. The organization is a leading group in advocacy at the state and national levels and is instrumental in lobbying for medical coverage for ART procedures, medical research, adoption benefits, and access to all family-building options. The organization's website is a wealth of knowledge for those interested in learning more about ART and infertility with articles, videos, fact sheets, interviews, and links to other resources.

Fertile Action

An empowering story of a cancer survivor turned ART advocate is Alice Crisci, founder of the organization Fertile Action (http://www.fertileaction.org). Fertile Action is a nonprofit working to ensure that fertile women, touched by cancer, can become mothers. The organization provides education, advocacy, support, and financial aid and discounted fertility preservation assistance to those in need to utilize ART.

Alice Crisci founded Fertile Action as the My Vision Foundation in 2008, a few weeks after she was diagnosed with breast cancer at thirty-one years old. Struck by the limited resources available for young women with cancer and fueled by her personal experience funding her fertility preservation by stretching the limits of her credit card, Crisci vowed to protect the dreams that women touched by cancer have of their future.

In 2009, Crisci and her board of directors realized they gained so much traction in the fertility preservation field that it was necessary to rename My Vision Foundation as Fertile Action, and they joined Community Partners, a nonprofit organization for fiscal sponsorship. Crisci now runs My Vision as a for-profit consumer products company that also houses My Vision PhotoTherapy, providing photography sessions to women prior to body-altering surgeries. One hundred percent of the proceeds from the photography sessions fund scholarships for Fertile Action and My Vision Photography. In 2014, Crisci welcomed her fertility preservation miracle son, Dante, into the world. He is her inspiration for helping other survivors realize the joys of motherhood

Men Having Babies (MHB)

According to Ron Poole-Dayan, executive director and board member of Men Having Babies (MHB), gay men as a category face the most obstacles in their quest for parenting, including biological, legal, and social constraints, as well as significantly higher financial costs. A wide survey conducted by MHB found that gay parents spend an average of $110,000 on their parenting journey and that many underestimated the required costs by ten thousand dollars or more. It is not surprising that about 50 percent of intended parents have expressed an interest in financial assistance for people who cannot afford the entire process.

MHB has grown from a program that ran at the NYC LGBT Center starting in 2005 to an independent nonprofit organization dedicated to providing gay biological fathers and fathers-to-be with educational and financial support. Now with over three thousand couples and singles worldwide, MHB provides invaluable support to prospective gay fathers, including ratings of surrogacy agencies and fertility clinics, seminars, exhibits and workshops in New York, Chicago, Brussels, San Francisco, and Tel Aviv.

One of MHB's main goals is to promote the affordability of surrogacy and other parenting-related services for gay men. The organization works toward this objective through direct financial assistance, the encouragement of cost transparency, and customer feedback. Other invaluable services of MHB include:

- The Gay Parenting Assistance Program, providing prospective fathers who cannot afford the expenses involved with parenting through surrogacy with over a million dollars' worth of cash grants, discounts, and free services from over fifty leading service providers.
- In an effort to promote cost transparency and affordability, MHB embarked in 2012 on creating "SurrogacyAdvisor"—the world's only source for peer reviews and ratings of surrogacy agencies and IVF clinics. The initiative is facilitated by hundreds of surveys from surrogacy parents, gay and straight, from around the world. Summary tables list several dozen leading surrogacy agencies (menhavingbabies.org/agencies) and fertility clinics (menhavingbabies.org/clinics) in a descending order based on their overall ratings, and with a few major performance indicators: how many of our members used them, overall satisfaction, first cycle success rates (for clinics), average overall journey costs (agencies), and duration of the process. This detailed feedback and real cost figures already proved invaluable to numerous prospective parents, and helped them save tens of thousand of dollars by identifying affordable effective providers and creating downward pricing pressure.
- Deciphering surrogacy costs, MHB developed a surrogacy budgeting system that includes a checklist of all possible cost components, and a table with cost ranges for each component, subcategory, and overall journey. (See Chapter 3.)

- Facilitating access to a wider set of options, MHB also offers a comprehensive provider directory (menhavingbabies.org/directory) with about 150 providers from across the world (fertility clinics, surrogacy agencies, egg donation agencies, and law firms). The provider directory also includes a link to a referral form that allows prospective parents to contact dozens of providers in one step.

International Council on Infertility Information Dissemination (INCIID)

The International Council on Infertility Information Dissemination (http://www.inciid.org) is a nonprofit organization that helps individuals and couples explore their family-building options. INCIID provides an independent voice for consumers on diagnosis, treatment, and prevention of infertility as well as those considering adoption or child-free lifestyle. INCIID was created by infertile patients who have fought their way through the challenge and won.

INCIID provides current information and immediate support regarding the diagnosis, treatment, and prevention of infertility and pregnancy loss and offers guidance to those considering adoption or child-free lifestyles. INCIID's advisory board includes internationally renowned experts to ensure that the information on the site is accurate with the latest diagnostic and treatment protocols. INCIID also offers an IVF scholarship designed to help individuals and couples with financial and medical need for IVF but who are without insurance to cover the expense and who are childless (some exceptions apply).

Conclusion

Well, there you have it. If you've made it to this point, you've learned a lot more than most people will ever know about ART and how to navigate the process. You've hopefully learned whether it's right for you, how to get started, what it ought to cost, what your expectations should reasonably be, and how to reconcile successes and setbacks. Most importantly, we think, you should know that no matter what the outcome, *you are not alone!* There are tens of thousands of others in your shoes as you read this, with hopes and dreams *just like yours!*

Please keep in touch with the authors via their very informative website, which you can find at http://www.IVFConsumerGuide.com. There you will be able to interact with the authors, ask questions, and read the latest articles and cases on the subject of ART. Visit regularly, as resources are likely to be in continual development, and updates to the law and medical procedures will be reported as they occur.

The authors would be delighted to speak to *your group!* Information on engaging the authors, either individually or as a team—for personal appearances, keynote presentations, and book-signings—is available on the website.

Index